LONGCHAMP

Graphic Design: Delphine Delastre and Rosemarie Auberson
Illustrations: Karine Modeste
Correction: Renaud Bezombes
Translation: I.D.O. Paris21

LONGCHAMP

MARIE AUCOUTURIER
PHOTOGRAPHS BY PHILIPPE GARCIA

Éditions
de La Martinière

CONTENTS

A STORY OF LOVE…
A STORY OF A FAMILY…

BY THE NAME OF CASSEGRAIN.
A MILL ON THE LONGCHAMP RACETRACK UNITED THEM
FOREVER BY LENDING ITS NAME TO THE BRAND.
IN THE BEGINNING, DELUXE LEATHER-COVERED PIPES.
THEN THE COMPANY FOUND ITS WAY FORWARD
BY BUILDING A BRIDGE BETWEEN THE EQUESTRIAN WORLD
AND THE WORLD OF TRAVEL.
THE MERGER OF THESE TWO WORLDS GAVE IT A DEFINITE
INTERNATIONAL DIMENSION.
THEN THE "NOUVELLE VAGUE" APPEARED ON THE SCENE…
SOPHIE, JEAN AND OLIVIER – A VIRTUAL REBIRTH.
JEAN'S PERSPECTIVE, OLIVIER'S GENEROSITY,
SOPHIE'S PASSION…
JEAN'S STRENGTH, SOPHIE'S INTUITION…
FOR MY THREE FRIENDS
TRADITION GOES HAND IN HAND
WITH IMAGINATION OPTIMISM WITH FAITH
VISION WITH MAGIC.

HAPPY ANNIVERSARY!

BABETH DJIAN

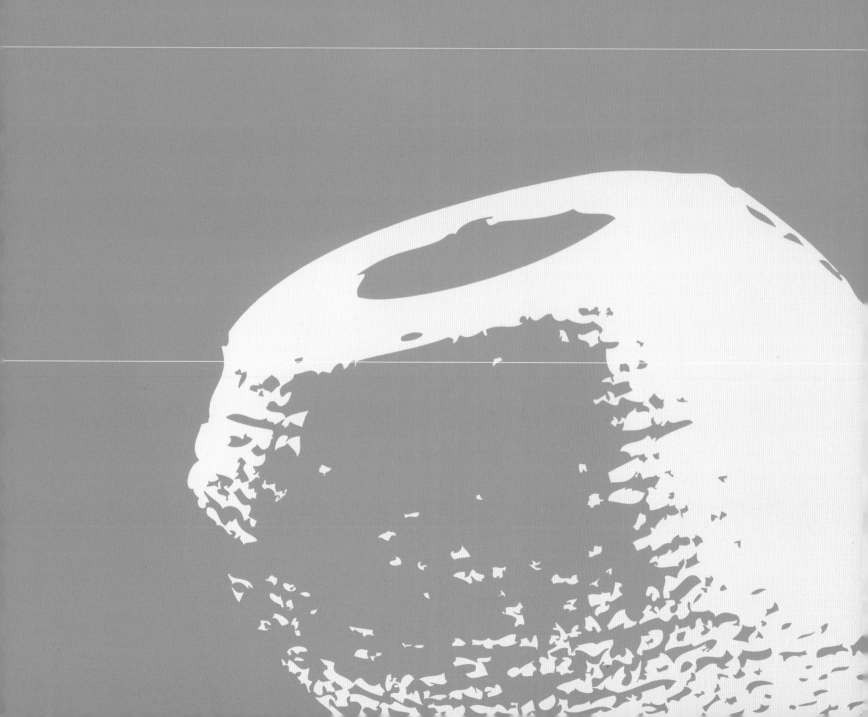

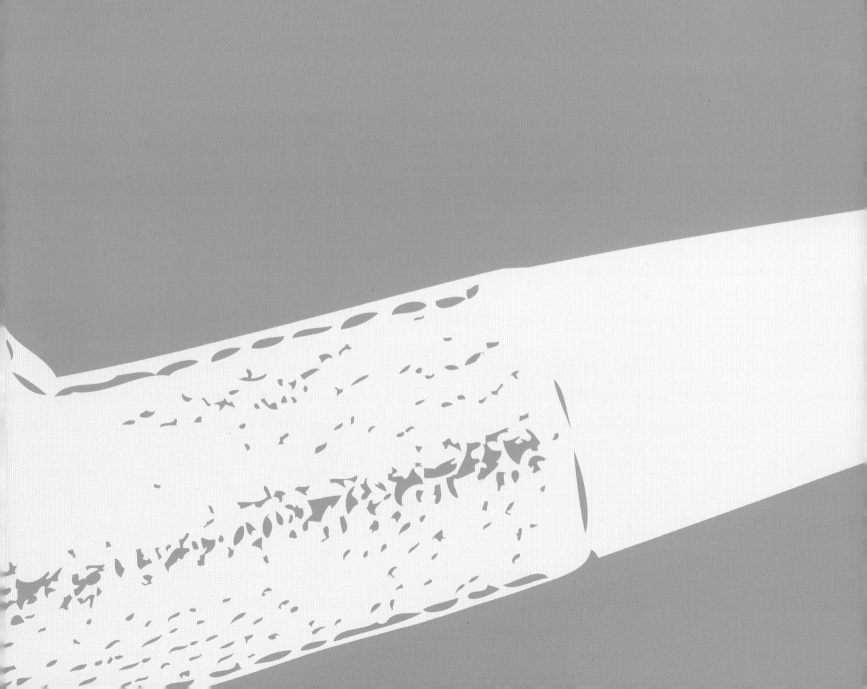

August 1940. End of the exodus. At 9 *bis* Boulevard Poissonnière, the finely fitted copper and mahogany shop was being polished up for the return of Gaston Cassegrain's son, Jean. The building's façade was proudly adorned with the ornamental golden letters – *Au Sultan* –, evoking a *Thousand and One Nights* in the very heart of Paris. It's true that Gaston always had a passion for the art of naming – beginning with his own name. Undoubtedly feeling that his first name, Raymond, didn't entirely suit him, he chose to call himself Gaston. Gaston Cassegrain had a nice ring to it and was certainly a much better choice than Raymond. No doubt his choice was intended as a little jab at high-flown manners. He was a real model for Jean. Force of character was definitely more than a legend in the family. And even though Jean's marriage to his second cousin, Renée, was frowned upon by some, this didn't bother the young man a bit. After all, true love knows no bounds. Neighsayers should mind their own business: for him the marriage of a Cassegrain to a Cassegrain was a storybook tale to tell the grandchildren!

For the moment, Jean decided to return from La Réole where he was studying at the École Polytechnique. The young man, who was extremely curious about everything, proved his resourcefulness as a true jack of all trades – working as a chemist-oenologist one day, a pig breeder the next, a Christmas-tree seller during the holidays and a teaching assistant at the Polytechnic Institute, among countless other pursuits. And to top it all off, he had a mastery of German and English still uncommon at the time. Jean gave off an aura of something bigger to come. He had the potential of a great man in the making.

In the end, he settled down comfortably in Paris with Renée and their four children in the building above the store, ready and willing to take over his father's business – a business rich with promise: in fact, the establishment known as the Sultan was one of the capital's rare "civettes", a nickname for tobacco shops in France. At the time, tobacco had a sun-ripened aura and taste, which was nothing more than a dream for most of the city during the war. Every month, a horse-drawn wagon delivered between 400 and 500 kilos of "brown gold" to the shop on Boulevard Poissonnière. Since each inhabitant was entitled to two packs of cigarettes every other week, the civette quickly had a lot of business. It was frequented by the regulars of the Boulevard's many shows, and one might run into Tino Rossi or Charles Trenet between acts at the A.B.C. – the nearby music hall.

The phenomenon gained in intensity when Paris was liberated in 1944. The Boulevard Poissonnière address became one of those not-so-well-kept secrets known to increasing numbers of allied troops who came to the shop to buy tobacco and smoking accessories.

And surprisingly enough, it turned out that the servicemen were crazy about pipes. Inventory was soon depleted, and replenishing it was no easy matter. While his colleagues calmly placed their written orders with the pipemakers of Saint-Claude,

Preceding page: Billiard-shaped Longchamp Pipe, sheathed in black crocodile.

Opposite, left: Gaston Cassegrain in front of the civette *Au Sultan* in the 1930s.
Top right: Jean and Renée Cassegrain in 1935.
Lower left: The counter of the civette.
Lower right: Renée Cassegrain and her shop assistants in front of the civette.

Following page: Apple-shaped Longchamp pipe with Saddle stem, sheathed in tobacco-colored calf suede, with its Hercules pipe-holder.

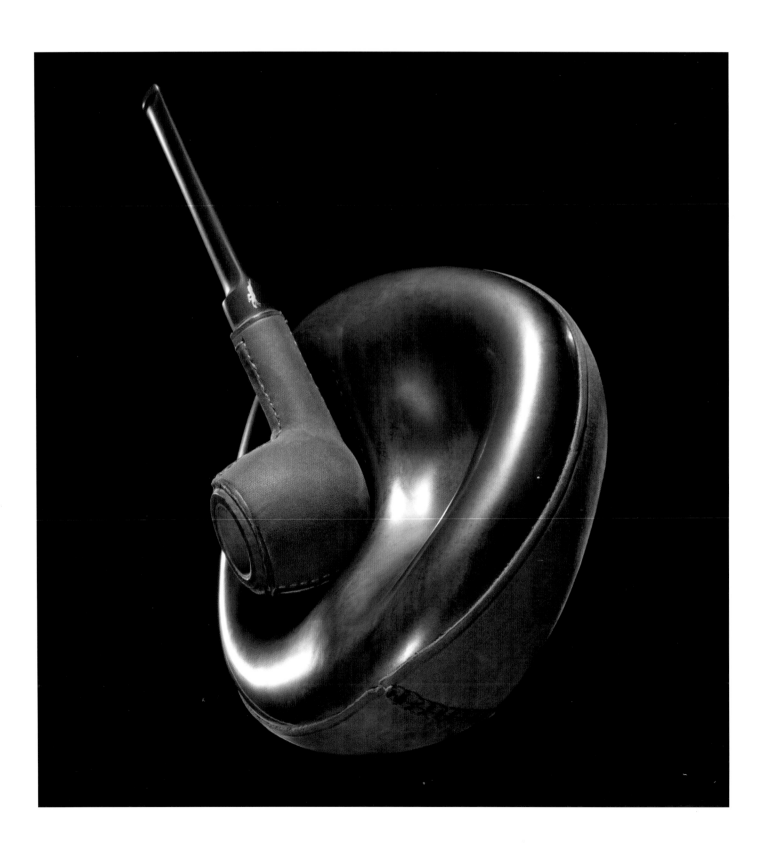

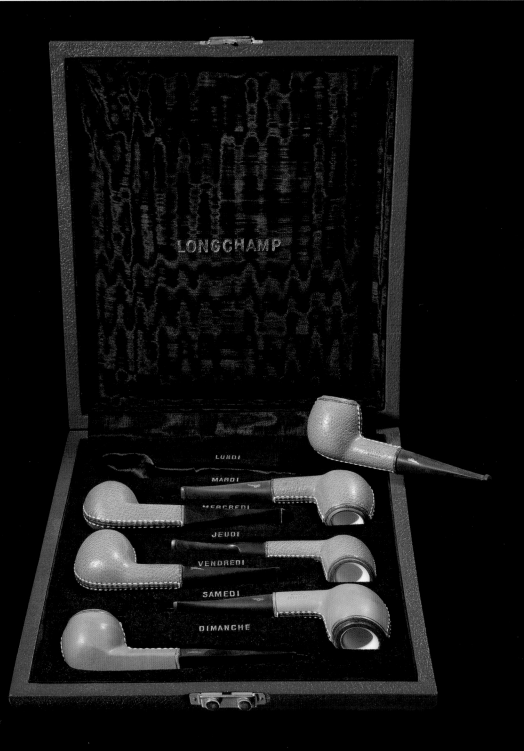

Preceding page: Semainier of coral leather pipes lined
with black taffeta.
Seven half-meerschaum pipes sheathed in natural calfskin
or goat leather with pigskin grain.

Opposite: Desktop pipe-holder made from black calfskin and
metal gilded with fine gold. Straight Billiard-shaped pipes
sheathed in taupe calf suede.

Below: Catalog from the 1960s.
An advertisement for the *Lady*, a pipe for ladies.

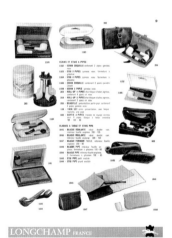

Jean decided it was the right time to try his luck with a more original approach. At the wheel of his trusty automobile – a front-wheel drive with the registration number 1014RN6 – he took off in the pursuit of the pipemakers of the Jura. And he came back with a satisfied gleam in his eye, the car overflowing with pipes from the trunk spilling into the rear seats. His shop was the best-stocked in Paris. Like a trail of powder, pipe sales exploded. Servicemen spread the word. Sitting on their heels, they patiently awaited the opening of the civette each morning, in an orderly line that occasionally stretched all the way to the Rue du Sentier.

It was inevitable that when the soldiers began to leave Paris in 1945, the civette's business felt the shock. But Jean Cassegrain had other ideas up his sleeves. So what if his pipes were no longer selling like hotcakes? Jean wasn't concerned a bit. His solution: the Sultan would sell even finer pipes – pipes that couldn't be found anywhere else. He came up with a brilliant idea – out of the blue: since certain smoking accessories, such as cigarette cases were often sheathed in leather, why not sell leather-sheathed pipes? A decidedly chic product, which, in the end, proved to be truly visionary!
This innovation marked the debut of Cassegrain products in the annals of luxury. Nothing but the finest leathers were used, from calfskin to kidskin, including such exotic leathers as horsehair and crocodile. The shop's name, *Au Sultan*, had never so perfectly epitomized the establishment. Cassegrain bought his pipes at Saint-Claude and entrusted them to Paris's most skilled craftsmen for sheathing. The degree of craftsmanship required for the fabrication of such a small object – often underestimated – is staggering. The finishing stage, in particular, is a highly meticulous process. The shop's success was immediate. Yet it was simply a teaser for what was to come: the leather-covered pipe would soon outgrow over-the-counter sales. Jean foresaw that it was time to start supplying his colleagues and enter the wholesale trade. Spurred on by his success, our ambitious young man founded his own company the same year – in 1948 – and called it, quite simply, *Jean Cassegrain et Compagnie*. He didn't know it yet, but he had just given birth to what would become a legendary institution in fine French leather goods.

The business was organized very rapidly and the various tasks were divvied out spontaneously. Madame Cassegrain ran the civette, where the gentlemen of the neighborhood bought their Christmas cigars. The shop also sold S.T. Dupont lighters, supplied by Mr. Tissot Dupont, one of Jean's closest friends. At the *Sultan* they sold for 620 francs, in handsome gold or silver-plated versions. And, as the epitome of refinement, Jean added a personal touch by having them personalized by the lacquerer Dinh Van with the initials of their proud owners. After all, a gentleman's elegance should never be left to chance.

Jean Cassegrain was the first to create leather-covered pipes. The craftsmen entrusted with this task developed a meticulous technique directly drawn from the saddler's trade.

The craftsmen prepared the half-form of the pipe from vegetable-tanned leather, which was then soaked in water so that it would take on the curves of the pipe. Once it was shaped, the leather was over-cut in the middle to complete the finishing process, then sewn together by hand when dry using two needles drawn simultaneously.

1972: Elvis Presley and one of his many Longchamp pipes, given to him by his friend Janelle McComb.

And not one to ignore the ladies, he introduced the *Lady*, a pipe designed especially for women with strong personalities, inclined to follow in the footsteps of George Sand. The budding entrepreneur also installed a leather cutting shop under the eves of the building in order to supply his craftsmen promptly and efficiently. Since entrepreneurship came natural to him, he presented his goods in the display windows of the finest hotels and also sold his pipes in the American army's PX stores. At the dawn of the Cold War, the Post Exchange arrangement represented an incalculable number of points of sale, since the PX's were directly linked to military bases. Thanks to this pioneering sales network, Longchamp products were sold in 102 countries as early as 1960! This amounted to a very substantial market, which Jean, with his legendary curiosity, covered in person: Tokyo, Guam, Dallas – no corner of the globe was overlooked. As early as 1955, he began exporting Longchamp products to Japan, engaging the services of a general agent several years later. The international dimension of the business always seemed crucial to him. And when the corners of the globe still seemed out of his reach, the pipes themselves served as ambassadors. A French delegation of the CGT labor federation offered one to Stalin during a trip to Russia; and Elvis Presley, among other celebrities, was a fervent collector.

Jean also created a sales team to promote his products. He hired Gilbert Batisse in 1949, then Peter Cussac in 1953, two legendary Longchamp figures: the first established brand in the south of France, before this task was entrusted to Jean's son, Philippe, in 1991; and the second assumed responsibility for Longchamp's international development for nearly forty years.

Concerned that his team might not have enough to keep them busy, Jean didn't hesitate to fill their bags with a few other trinkets purchased here and there. The company was even known to sell plaster poodles, offering a model for everyone's taste: black or white; small, medium or large; lying down, seated, standing, you name it. The company founder was never known to lack humor. Even though he began producing leather articles, such as lambskin tobacco pouches and cigarette cases, he continued to be obsessed by the idea of sheathing objects in leather. The poodles quickly give way to ceramic products of all types, such as ashtrays or leather-cased tobacco jars. In 1952, he opened a second Sultan shop in Nice, on Rue Massena. From the capital to the south of France, it became the ultimate in chic to offer gifts signed Longchamp.

But Jean Cassegrain was gradually drawn to the exploration of new horizons. His heart was already being drawn to far-away adventures.

After working at the Sultan selling pipes during the Liberation of France by Allied troops, Jean Cassegrain's brother-in-law was assigned to make sales rounds throughout France. He visited every corner of the country in his Peugeot 201, before assuming responsibility for the procurement of leather for the company. He remained in this role for the better part of his life.

Longchamp pipes are heat-proof: an advertising poster designed by Turenne Chevallereau in 1951.

Following pages: Insulated ice bucket in the shape of an elephant's foot. Ceramic sheathed in tawny calfskin. Ashtray/pipe-holder in tortoiseshell ceramic, sheathed in Havana calf suede.

Opposite: Passport covers in box calf with gold leafing.

Below: Gilding stamp used for hot iron branding of the Longchamp logo.

Memories of Longchamp…

By Alain Cassegrain

After working at the *Sultan* selling pipes during the Liberation of France by Allied troops, Jean Cassegrain's brother-in-law was assigned to make sales rounds throughout France. He visited every corner of the country in his Peugeot 201, before assuming responsibility for the procurement of leather for the company. He remained in this role for the better part of his life.

"One day, Jean came up with the idea of creating leather passport covers. We produced a case for French passports, crafted in fine leather, beautifully embossed with a gold-leaf imprint. Jean then decided to produce covers for other countries as well. I went around to all the embassies to collect old passport covers, which we intended to reproduce in leather. Some of them refused, of course – the British authorities, in particular. Certain insignias were superb – the Persian Empire's, for example. We had the leather gilded by a craftsman who worked with gold-leaf, using a hand gilding press, which was standard practice in the nineteenth century. It was a touch that appealed a great deal to customers. Delion, a hatter located in the fashionable Rue du Faubourg Saint Honoré, sold them in incredible quantities!"

The Longchamp *Mystique*

From the very beginning, Jean's leather-cased pipes were stamped *Longchamp*. A strange name for a pipe, you may say… Where did it come from?

The name *Cassegrain* was already used by a cousin for a motorcycle business in Orleans. A mill appeared next to the trade name, in tribute to the milling industry from which *casse-grain* (grain mill) was derived. Since Jean couldn't use his family name for his own business, the mill logo stimulated his imagination in a different way: at the very end of the Longchamp racetrack loomed one of the last mills left in Paris. This equestrian universe, along with the saddler's expertise in leather casing, finally convinced him that the *Longchamp* brand name had potential. It also had the merit of being easily pronounceable in all languages, which appealed to his entrepreneurial spirit.

In order to play this equestrian card to his best advantage, Jean commissioned a logo depicting a spirited horse from the illustrator, Turenne Chevallereau. Chevallereau drew his inspiration from nineteenth century engravings, in which the appearance of the racing horse is elongated like a slender branch reaching for the sky, with all four hooves in the air – a spectacular, ethereal levitation bordering on the dream world of poetry.

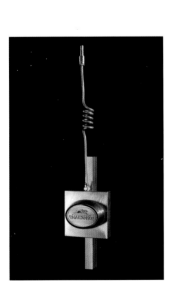

Jean Cassegrain invented a magnetic leather-covered cigarette case for automobiles of the 1950s, which could be magnetically attached to the vehicle's dashboard. He then created a metal display stand for the presentation of this object in window displays, which needed a bit of staging to achieve the full effect. So he borrowed a friend's convertible and drove out to Longchamp stadium with a photographer in search of a backdrop for the display. The two men fell under the charm of the famous Longchamp mill, which they decided to include in the shot.
At the time, cars did not have built-in ashtrays; and that was how Longchamp came to produce magnetic leather-covered ashtrays.

EXPORT

J. CASSEGRA

20 RUE S^{T.} FL

TENBERG 91-76

PA

Nice, 1948, under a blazing sun. Seated at the terrace of a café with his brother-in-law, Alain, Jean Cassegrain took a deep drag on his cigarette – nothing out of the ordinary for the owner of a civette, but a bit of a cliché for this epitome retailer of smoking accessories.

That day, however, the acrid taste of a post-war cigarette bothered him… and he put it out in an ashtray. It was to be his last – the infamous last cigarette. End of story.

No doubt that moment in Nice stuck in the mind of the brilliant entrepreneur. A sort of premonition suggested to him the imminent decline of smoking, along with its array of accessories. The tradition of tobacco pouches had not totally disappeared from the streets of Paris. But Jean felt that it was time to start thinking about the future. While presenting his collections at the Foire de Paris (annual Paris market), and then at the *Semaine du Cuir* (Leather Week) in 1949, his young company began to associate with specialized leather-goods dealers and retailers. Once committed to a venture, Jean was not one to skimp. It had to be the *Foire de Paris* or nothing. It was there that he met with the world's elite, from Vincent Auriol to René Coty, who had come to celebrate the brilliance of French savoir-faire. Over the years, it became a not-to-be-missed event. Each generation of the family successively experienced the feverish atmosphere of the stands and the fair's good-natured atmosphere.

The trade exhibitions kept on building in intensity. Jean sent his son, Philippe, to play the role of ambassador to trade shows all over the world. In such distant destinations as Milan, Tokyo and California, the young man energetically contributed to building Longchamp's reputation. At the age of 20, Philippe took off to exhibit the company's products at the New York Coliseum, with seven bags, no less, under his arms, jam packed with collapsible shelving units and products manufactured by the company – in short, everything needed to create an authentic Longchamp stand in the land of Uncle Sam.

For his part, Jean gradually introduced small leather goods into his collections. Men's wallets and clutch cases popped up here and there, along with several larger items, including a garment bag in supple lambskin – now considered the ancestor of Longchamp luggage. The *smoking* line gradually diminished, hanging on until 1978, when the last pipes were listed in the catalogue. After producing nearly a million pipes, Longchamp finally closed a memorable chapter in its history.

This new direction was accompanied by a major leap forward in the company's method of manufacturing its products. Jean understood that it was urgent to develop his company's production capacity, which was still based for the most

Preceding page: Cigarette cases crafted from lizard, grained goat and sealskin.

Opposite, top: *Jean Cassegrain et Compagnie* stand at the Paris Fair in the 1950s.
Lower left: Jean Cassegrain (center) and Gilbert Batisse (right) at the Paris Fair.
Lower right: Jean Cassegrain (right) and his daughter Brigitte (extreme right) present a Longchamp semainier to French President René Coty, as he visited the Paris Fair on June 3, 1954.

Below: Leather goods catalog from the 1960s.

maroquinerie
monsieur

voyages
week-end

part in Paris, with production handled by the home-based artisans of the early years. He therefore approached several suppliers, including Lepage, a tanner specializing in horsehair leather. Lepage knew a couple of artisans, Émile and Marie-Louise Allet, who made beautiful leather bags for ladies in Segré near Angers. The workshop employed a dozen women with exceedingly dexterous fingers, and was delighted to expand its business. Cassegrain decided to give them a try. He asked them to produce a card holder, giving them the pre-cut pieces of leather during the Paris Fair. Jean-François, his second son, was astounded: "When Mr. Allet arrived at the Fair, we gave him nearly fifty kilos of leather and materials which he immediately carried off with him. I can't imagine how; the load was so heavy, he must have superhuman strength! One thing is sure: he disappeared right into the metro entrance. I was filled with admiration!"

The card holders were a success…, and Cassegrain had met his preferred supplier. The couple worked our of their home, surrounded by a growing number of women workers, who proved to be experts with python and cobra, and virtuosos of the stitching needle and leather treatment. The Longchamp orders kept on increasing, and space was rapidly in short supply. Even the master bedroom was requisitioned for work! Mr. Allet mentioned the problem to Jean, who suggested that he open a large workshop in the center of Segré. The offer impressed the tradesman, who became the head of the company's first production unit in 1959. This gleaming new production shop gave the company a new impetus, to Cassegrain's delight. Even so, he didn't abandon his craftsmen in Paris, who had helped build the company from the ground up. Loyalty had always been a key element of the company's philosophy. The transition was accomplished gradually, and Cassegrain invited any of his willing Parisian workers to join the venture in Anjou.

Preceding pages: Enameled calf skins ready for cutting, to be used for the production of *Légende* handbags. Factory girls working at a table in the first Segré workshop, constructed in 1959.

Below, left: Mrs. Poirier, a seamstress at the Allet workshops, stitches leather. Below, right: A handbag model produced by the Allet workshops before they began working for Longchamp.

Above: Entrance to the offices of *Jean Cassegrain et Compagnie*, rue Saint-Fiacre in Paris.
Sketch by Turenne Chevallereau for the fitting-out of the company's offices.
Right: Showroom for Longchamp products in the rue Saint-Fiacre.

Turenne Chevallereau, master draftsman

The problem of putting Jean's ideas down on paper was a delicate subject. With furrowed eyebrows, the craftsmen painstakingly tried to decipher the boss's intentions on paper. No one doubted his genius, but he was far from being an ace at the drawing board. It was not really a problem for small leather goods, where the models could be developed directly in the shop by the workers. But when he decided to attack larger projects, Jean had to redouble his efforts.

That was when it was decided to introduce Turenne Chevallereau – who had already produced advertisements for the company – into the equation. The renowned illustrator practiced his art just about everywhere: at the Paris Fair, with his sketches for the pipe display stand, in the decoration of the company's offices and showroom for example; his deft, creative hand left its mark throughout the company. Until the day Jean surprised his son, Philippe, pencil in hand. The young man showed artistic promise…, and that was the beginning of a creative makeover.

The Foire de Paris and the Semaine du Cuir: two annual events at which the company's loyal customers were welcomed
By Jean-François Cassegrain

"At the time, the Paris Fair did not have an onsite food service system, like today. Madame Cassegrain, my mother, therefore decided to organize lunches for our customers, which were always lively and energetic affairs. Everyone assisted her. I served tables with my sister Brigitte, while my brother Dominique warmed up the food before it was served. We offered our customers a delightful, refreshing pause right in the middle the chaotic fair. Some of our guests were dubious, convinced that there was a monetary motive behind it all, and that they would pay at the end of the meal. One day, when things were set up to resemble a bistro, a female customer sat down at the table and ordered champagne, which naturally, we served her immediately. Then, when she had selected her various courses among the choices we were offering that day and finished her meal, she asked for the check. She couldn't have been more embarrassed when we explained that she was our guest. The attention Madame Cassegrain lavished on our guests was without equal."

Below: Brigitte and Jean-François Cassegrain (right) present a selection of Longchamp products on the set of the TV show "Télé Paris", December 1960.

Opposite: Philippe Cassegrain in 1957.

Memoirs of Monsieur Philippe, the timeless young man

Philippe Cassegrain joined the venture at a very early age. With his many years of experience – from the time when he would lend a hand after school until he assumed the position of chief executive – he accumulated a veritable treasure trove of tales about the company, which he takes great pleasure in telling in a slightly mischievous manner.

"From the moment my father decided to get in involved in the wholesale trade, there was plenty of work for everyone. We were all put to work, so to speak. When I was not at school, my job was to run the small press that was used to stamp the inside of the cigarette cases with the Longchamp logo. I was also responsible for collecting raw materials for the artisans working at home. I quickly became the head of the department – taking on my brothers as subcontractors. I was also responsible for restocking the showcases of the luxury hotels, and I made regular runs to the *Ritz*, the *Ambassador* and the *Claridge*, among others. I was so successful, my father decided to reward me with a brand new Vespa scooter. That was in 1953, and I was 16 at the time. It was a real surprise. I was expecting a basic little moped at the most!

My parents sent me all over the world when I was still very young. I began working in a transport agency in Birmingham; then, at the age of 16, I was sent off on a tour of Africa. My father put me on board the boat in London and picked me up two months later in Marseille. That was the year of the Queen of England's coronation; I traveled with a group of scouts from South Africa who had come to England for the coronation. Everyone knew me on the boat.

When I got back, my father sent me out to prospect the regions of France that no one else wanted to cover. I was only 17 at the time, and didn't yet have my driver's license! So the company's delivery man drove me himself. My territory included the least desirable destinations: Orleans, Libourne, La Bourboule among others."

The skilled know-how of the Segré workshops helped the company make a smooth transition from world of smoking accessories to a broader range of leather goods. Little by little, the well-oiled machine gained momentum. Jean, assisted by his son Philippe, was finally free to develop the new product range.

International courier

As an advocate of open dialogue and cooperation between nations, Jean Cassegrain decided to send his son Philippe on a scouting trip to the United States and Canada. The young man crossed the Atlantic for the first time in 1956, and then once again in 1957. He crisscrossed North America by Greyhound bus and slept at local YMCAs. His destinations included New York, Boston, Ottawa, Detroit, Toronto, Cleveland, Chicago, Milwaukee, Saint-Louis, Indianapolis, Cincinnati, Dayton, Pittsburgh, Washington, Philadelphia and Atlantic City.

During these various expeditions, many letters were exchanged with his father, in which the founder of Longchamp gave his son meticulously detailed sales missions.

When he arrived at the New York YMCA, Philippe found a letter waiting for him reminding him not to forget to stay in touch with his customers in France: "Start working on your postcards as soon as you arrive. Make a list of everyone who should receive one. Remember your customers first. Certain customers might even appreciate receiving two […]. Don't be afraid of overdoing it."

A week later, Jean sent his son a reminder through the post: "Don't forget to send a card to all your customers, because once you've left New York, things will start moving so fast you won't have the time to do everything."

Philippe was also reminded to call on Longchamp's prestigious American customers: "Don't forget to pay a visit to Mr. Kaufman, at Mark Cross or Mr. Berlin, if you can't see him […]. I'm counting on you to call on all the important people in New York, and some of them more than once […]. Try to send us some orders […]. I'm sure you're doing your best, but don't be afraid to be assertive."

During these visits, one of Philippe's tasks was to provide his customers with an update on their orders. "Saks hasn't received their delivery yet, we'll deliver tomorrow or Monday at the latest. Maybe you should see Mr. Sullerton to apologize for the delay," his father pointed out. Adding without transition: "We're sending out the Marshall Fields order; Mr. Cussac [*Longchamp's export manager*] will keep you informed. Don't forget to visit VL and Anthony while you're there […]; they might be interested since they've already carried our pipes. I think there are also five or six tobacconists in Chicago."

Cassegrain senior hadn't forgotten his son's talent for drawing either, asking him to send back some sketches of his trip.

Opposite: Souvenirs of Philippe Cassegrain's first trip to the United States in 1956.

FUMEZ
LA PIPE
LONGCHAMP

REPUBLIQUE
FRANÇAISE
★0765

23 VII 56   ═PARIS-48═

To await arrival

If not collected by
August 1st, forward
on to YMCA, West side
Branch, 5 W.63rd St.,
New York 23, N.Y.

M. Philippe Cassegrain

Young Men's Christian Association,

Central Branch

1736 G. Street,

N.W.

Washington 6

U. S. A.

PAR AVION
AIR MAIL

French Line

Cⁱᵉ Gˡᵉ TRANSATLANTIQUE

Siège Social

iquer ci-contre
cal sanitaire
uel que si le
ger en a payé
tant.

/

JPP JPP

LE HAVRE à   NE

uebot   FLANDRE
(ou tout autre qui lui sera substitué)

art du   14 JUIN 1956

MS ET PRÉNOMS COMPLETS DES PASSAGERS
tels qu'ils figurent sur les passeports

MR PHILIPPE CASSEGRAIN

COMPAGNIE GENERAL
TRANSATLANTIQUE

PARIS - 6, rue Auber

NEW YORK - 610, Fifth Av.   LONDON - 20, Cockspur St., SWI

BILLET DE PASSAGE
PASSAGE TICKET

Voir note importante au dos - See important Notice over

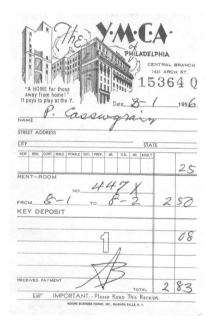

The Y·M·C·A·
of PHILADELPHIA
CENTRAL BRANCH
1421 ARCH ST.
15364 Q

"A HOME for those
away from home!"
It pays to play at the Y.

Date 8-1 1956

NAME P. Cassegrain

STREET ADDRESS

CITY   STATE

NEW	REN.	CONT.	MALE	FEMALE	SOC.	PREP.	JR.	O.B.	SR.	ADULT	
											25

RENT—ROOM   NO. 447 X

FROM 8-1 to 8-2   250

KEY DEPOSIT

1   08

TOTAL 283

☞ IMPORTANT: - Please Keep This Receipt.

MOORE BUSINESS FORMS, INC. NIAGARA FALLS, N. Y.

New York

THE
CONVENTION CITY
OF THE
WORLD
•

Undoubtedly satisfied with Philippe's work, Jean announced that Philippe would be handling the *US World Trade Fair*, a well-known international fair that was to be held in New York in April of 1957. "I understand you're disappointed to return eight days earlier than planned, but there's a lot of work to be done and do look on the bright side. There will very likely be another opportunity to send you to America for a month next April if you do well this time. Show us what you can do and it will be in the bag." Philippe did just that. He crossed the Atlantic once more in April 1957, with his bags full of samples, headed for the New York Coliseum. Just as he did the preceding year, his father provided him with detailed written instructions: "Always make appointments and be confident and firm […]. Don't leave any documents lying around that might interest the competition." The task confided to young Philippe represented a major challenge for Longchamp: "You will get newspaper and television coverage, which will be good advertising. I'm anxious to see how things go the first few days; this exhibition really could go either way. Don't forget to let me know what the competition is doing."

In these letters, Jean and his wife also provided their son with news of the family and of the company's business in Paris. From the letters, we learn that work on the family property in Ville-d'Avray was progressing rapidly, that Jean-François was working with his father during his school holiday, that Brigitte and Dominique had gone to the UK to study English, and so on. Jean, for his part, had ordered a new Citroën DS, which he was still impatiently awaiting; the delivery was slightly delayed, and he needed the car for his trip to the Offenbach Fair in Germany. Madame Cassegrain joked about this new acquisition: "It's here; the car has arrived. I would have preferred a Louis XV commode; it was the same price!" This jab did not diminish Renée's admiration for her husband: "Your father had a good order from Japan (around 6,000,000 francs, I think). He is overjoyed; and he deserves it, you know." Several weeks later, she added: "There's still lots of work here. We are way behind, due to the big export orders…, we have 10 or 12,000 pipes to deliver."

It was also by letter that Philippe learned that he had been drafted into the army. His father obtained a delay of several days, due to the fact that his son was out of the country. "My dear Philippe, this morning we received your travel orders; you are to report to the Dijon air base on May 4 […]. I told them you would be back on the 15th, but if you arrive on the 16th on the *Liberté*, that should be OK. You shouldn't count on spending more than an afternoon or evening in Paris though, since you will need to leave immediately for Dijon. The 8:10 morning train will get you there at 11:12."

Philippe returned from his American adventure to immediately join the French army. In all, he spent two and a half years in Algeria.

Below: The Longchamp stand designed by Philippe Cassegrain for the Universal Exposition at the New York Coliseum in 1957.

Each Sunday, people from Paris and the surrounding areas, decked out in their Sunday best, would make the weekly pilgrimage to the air terminal just outside the capital, where from the terrace they could watch planes take off. They were especially interested in modern-day aviation heroes such as Michèle Morgan and Jean Marais, who portrayed a love affair between hostess and pilot in the movie *Aux Yeux du Souvenir* (*Souvenir* in English).

Orly airport was a veritable field of dreams. Particularly since the opening of the South Terminal, inaugurated by General de Gaulle on February 24, 1961. The terminal drew more of a crowd than the Eiffel Tower – around a million visitors every year. France's finest new attraction had everybody talking. The French singer Gilbert Bécaud crooned *Dimanche à Orly* (Sunday at Orly) on airwaves throughout the land…

This infatuation with Orly did not surprise Jean Cassegrain. His sharp eye had already spotted the era's fascination for all things modern. Once again, he had taken the pulse of an entire era, and shrewdly decided to associate his company with the new terminal's future shopping mall.

Those close to him were shocked: "You can't be serious! How can you expect to sell luggage at an airport? Passengers will never buy bags! You're doomed to failure!"

Jean didn't budge an inch. Maybe his idea was preposterous, but he stuck to his guns: his company would sell bags at Orly – no ifs, ands or buts about it –, not only in public areas, but also in the area subject to customs authority, in order to reach as many people as possible. It's true that he had been tinkering with the idea of organizing his own distribution network for the last several years. The link with travel seemed all the more persuasive to him in that he had already tested the waters. Since the 1950s, Longchamp products had been sold on transatlantic liners, appealing to passengers' taste for luxury in the shops of such liners as the *Flandre* or the *Ile-de-France*. There was no doubt in his mind, travel, whether by sea or air, seemed to whet the stylish shopper's appetite for luxury goods.

These early stirrings of large-scale development offer a unique perspective on the arrival of some new players at Longchamp – or rather one main player: the Cassegrain family itself. They all fell into step behind Jean as the leader of the venture. United around the patriarch, each family member found his or her place. The brand's success at Orly's commercial counters marked the launch of its distribution throughout the world. As key players in this epic tale, the four Cassegrain children were involved from the beginning in the early stages of this fledgling retail venture. Brigitte, "father's little darling" as her brother Philippe affectionately called her, was designated to work at the boutique in

Preceding page: Cabin bag on rollers in tawny drummed calfskin.

Opposite: The Paris Orly Airport's first floor concourse during the 1960s. In the foreground, Dominique Cassegrain's boutique.

Longchamp
et nous Lc'est pour
Longtemps

Opposite: Photographer Daniel Aron's advertising campaign, 1996.

Below: Calfskin covers for pilot licenses and flight logs.

Following pages: *Pliage* bag in white drummed calfskin and *Spider* bag in mocha drummed calfskin.

the air terminal. But since she was still under 18, she didn't have her driver's license and therefore had no way of getting to Orly! In the meantime, Philippe manned the shop from 7 a.m. until 1 p.m., when a sales girl took over for the afternoon. The morning shift at Orly went like child's play for Philippe. He was all alone behind the cash register, Philippe treated his customers like royalty. The shop naturally sold Longchamp products, but also other brands such as rigid Samsonite bags, then at the cutting-edge of the avant-garde. People couldn't get enough of them. The Italians, with their penchant for elegant design, slipped the shop's address to their compatriots. Slowly but surely, Longchamp made a name for itself among the world's elite as they passed through Paris.

This privileged nomadic tribe intrigued Philippe. "We sold suitcases like hotcakes," he remembers, laughing out loud. How this was done is a mystery. It's true that there wasn't much competition at the time: Orly had a pharmacy, a newsstand and a perfume shop. At the dawn of *duty free* and a myriad of other temptations of all genres, the Cassegrains marked their territory before everyone else, never ceasing to broaden their influence in airports all over the world.

These purchases, too cumbersome for the plane's cabin, needed to be checked. So Philippe locked his cash register, left his customers to watch the

shop, and carted the empty bags away to the airlines' check-in counters. There were always a number of regular passengers who liked to stop and chat; the gentlemen would buy their wives a crocodile bag, and Philippe continued his incessant ballet up and down the corridors of Orly.

When Brigitte celebrated her 18th birthday, the changing of the guard finally took place. As a result, Philippe was free to devote himself entirely to the creation of Longchamp products, along with his father and his brother Jean-François. When Brigitte took the reigns, she was no less successful. Since these retail outlets were not yet exclusively devoted to Longchamp articles, the sales counters were branded *Dominique Cassegrain*, after the family's third son. The name *Brigitte Cassegrain* was not used since Jean refused to leave anything to chance. The first name *Dominique* can be either masculine or feminine and does not evoke a specific gender in the customer's mind. If Brigitte got married her last name would change and the brand would become obsolete.

The astounding quantities of bags sold at the Orly shop encouraged the Cassegrains to repeat the experiment when the new Roissy airport opened on the other side of Paris. A store in the public area and a shop in the area subject to customs were therefore opened in the brand new airport. The operation paid off handsomely. It was obvious that the young Brigitte had the makings of a successful businesswoman and enough energy to move mountains! She also had broad enough shoulders to juggle a host of new locations, including a shop at the Rungis Administrative Tower, a shop at the Hotel PLM Saint-Jacques, and a store on the Avenue de Suffren. Her multi-brand points of sale established the company's reputation at the four corners of Paris, enabling Longchamp to consolidate its foundations.

It was about then that Madame Cassegrain finally decided to leave the civette on the Boulevard Poissonnière. Her husband began to worry when he noticed that the shop's steady stream of customers never subsided. He was afraid the non-stop pace would wear Renée out. When the Cassegrains had lunch in their apartment on the fifth floor of the building, they sometimes forgot to lock the door of the civette. When they returned, they would often find a bunch of men in front of the cash desk, politely waiting for the shop to reopen. And if Monsieur Cassegrain wanted to speak with his wife in private, he had to close the shop to have a little peace and quiet. Madame Cassegrain clearly could not go on working at such a pace. So the *Sultan* was sold at the beginning of the 1960s. Renée, however, was far from content with her early retirement. Jean proposed that she open her own business – on the Champs-Élysées no less. Madame Cassegrain was tempted. In September 1968, she opened a boutique selling a range of different brands at number 84 of the fabulous avenue, and received all

Opposite: Longchamp catalog in the 1960s.

Below: Longchamp catalog cover in the 1960s.

Opposite: Jean Cassegrain at the Paris Fair.

the beautiful ladies out for a day of oh-so-chic window shopping. A small glass-front cabinet at the back of the shop displayed the crocodile wallets her customers were absolutely mad about. Just as her sister Françoise had lent a helping hand at the civette, and her brother Hervé had handled the logistics operations between Segré and Paris, her sister Marie-Pierre joined her in the Champs-Élysées boutique.

Even though each branch of the Cassegrain dynasty began to develop its own specific activities, there was never any question of splitting up the family. The building above the civette, which had its entrance on the Rue Saint-Fiacre, was nibbled away little by little to bring the joyous tribe together. The floors inhabited by the family formed a sort of link between the sales and creative departments. Jean's offices, where he worked with Philippe and Jean-François, were above the civette. The cellar was given over to the packaging and shipping department. Brigitte lived with her parents on the fifth floor, while the boys occupied the sixth floor. In the maid's rooms on the seventh floor, a small workshop was set up to produce prototypes. Reptile skins were also prepared there; they needed to be kept humid and attached to frames so they would not curl up.

And even though Jean eventually decided to settle down outside of Paris, the strong family ties were not weakened in the slightest. The family always gathered for Sunday lunches in the spacious house in Ville-d'Avray. During lunch, everyone talked about the past week, about their future plans, or the new source of leather someone had just discovered, which might be anywhere in the world. The words *papa* and *maman* were rarely heard: work habits took precedence. Even at table, Monsieur Cassegrain remained Monsieur Cassegrain. And the same applied to *Madame*.

After the meal, Jean adopted the tradition of bringing his family together in the office to distribute the weekly assignments. Everything was scrupulously documented in his notebooks, into which carbon sheets had been inserted to keep copies of all instructions. Notes were drawn up for everyone, and the instructions couldn't have been clearer. Someone might grumble a bit from time to time, but on Monday morning, it was "all business" for everyone.

However, these little notes scribbled left and right came to an abrupt and tragic end. On December 16, 1972, Jean Cassegrain was killed in an automobile accident on the Segré road. His children and grandchildren faced the daunting challenge of finding the strength to overcome the dark days that ensued.

"When Monsieur Cassegrain was killed, I lost my father and my boss," Jean-François remarked with dignity and modesty. Longchamp had suddenly lost its bearings. This was one of life's saddest and most painful challenges for the family. They refused to allow the cherished legacy to sink into oblivion.

Gilbert Bécaud : *Sundays in Orly (Dimanche à Orly)*, 1963

Staircase six, block twenty-one,

I live in a swell apartment

Which, if all goes well, my father

Will finish paying off in less than twenty years.

We have all the comforts,

An elevator and a bathroom,

We've got TV, a telephone

And a view of Paris in the distance.

On Sundays, my mother does housework

While my father, glued to the TV,

Watches sports so religiously

He doesn't even notice when I slip out the door

It's Sunday and I'm off to Orly.

At the airport you can watch the planes take off

For all the countries of the world,

All afternoon long… The stuff of dreams.

My ideas begin to run wild

When I go home at the end of the day.

At 7:05 every morning

Nicole and I take the metro.

Since we're still half-asleep, we don't say much,

And we each go off to our own jobs.

In the evening when I go to bed

I hear the Boeings singing on high.

I love my night birds

And plan to join them soon.

Yes, on Sunday I'm off to Orly.

At the airport you can watch the planes take off

For all the countries of the world,

For a whole lifetime… the stuff of dreams.

One day, from up there, block twenty-one

Will be nothing but a tiny, tiny little dot.

Words: Pierre Delanoë. Music: Gilbert Bécaud

© *Le Rideau Rouge / Universal Music Publishing MGB France*

Above: Gilbert Bécaud posing in front of an Air France
Super Constellation in the 1960s.

On your marks, get set, go!

Longchamp was not yet 25 years-old – an eligible young lady among luxury leather goods makers, who had lost her father and got people talking. Some whispered that the brand was finished. The Cassegrain children though, refused to give up ground to competitors. Philippe, Jean-François, Brigitte and Dominique were united in their belief that Longchamp would survive and prosper.

By way of inheritance, they acquired a legacy – whose future was up to them. Uncertainty was not a problem for the company's new directors: their early inclusion in the life of the company adequately prepared them. There was no bickering or squabbling... If the situation became a bit too tense, Madame Cassegrain knew perfectly well how to calm things down: "If you go on like that, I'll sell everything." Case closed – a consensus suddenly emerged.

A waltz-like rhythm gradually emerged – a waltz for eight hands, with four hands playing the swaying "ump-pah-pah" accompaniment of the company's distribution activities, while the other four played the soaring creative melody adorned with an occasional flourish of *pizzicati*... This fluidly moving score was faultlessly interpreted, gradually establishing Longchamp's reputation as a rising star in contemporary luxury. This was due in large part to the efforts of Brigitte – and the little horse with the allure of a proud steed, Dominique –, who charged ahead to conquer the globe with their network of multiple-brand boutiques. The company had definitively moved beyond smoking accessories and pungent-smelling tobacco shops. From now on, Longchamp concentrated on display windows of leather goods boutiques and department stores. As astute businessmen, Jean-François and Philippe closely monitored these retail activities. To increase the pace of expansion, they even created sales offices, such as the office created in New York's Empire State Building in 1982 – the same year Brigitte opened her own retail store on Madison Avenue. Nor did they hesitate to expand into Asia by joining forces with Johnny Shum, a Chinese agent with great influence in the region. Johnny Shum introduced Jean-François and Philippe to this new market, and inaugurated the first single-brand Longchamp shop in Hong Kong in 1979.

But Philippe and Jean-François primarily concentrated their efforts on the Longchamp product line. When Philippe was named the company's chief executive, he kept his head on his shoulders. Growth was the objective, but a revolution was out of the question. As their business expanded, the young managers noticed that ladies had become infatuated with handbags. They therefore decided to try to tap this growing market. Since 1971, the year he created his first woman's handbag, Philippe had been working on the idea of expanding into women's accessories. First of all, he toyed with the idea of reworking a toiletry case by adding a shoulder strap and two flaps. Unfortunately the working drawing of the object gave it a sober, masculine appearance. This transition to the handbag kept Philippe thin-

Preceding page: Duffel bag from the *LM* collection in chocolate embossed leather.

Below: Inauguration of the Longchamp boutique in Beijing, on May 15, 2008. Left to right: Johnny Shum, Sun Li, Patty Hou, Jean Cassegrain, Josie Ho et Shu Qi.

Opposite: Heat embossing and hot iron branding of the Longchamp logo in the 1970s.

Opposite: Squaremouth "doctor's bag" in chestnut *LM*
printed nylon with Shadow effect and calfskin leather details,
1976.

Below: Sketch of the first model of a lady's handbag, 1971.

Following pages: Black drummed calfskin beggar's bag.
White crocodile-embossed calfskins.

king. He continued working on it, adapting it to a wide range of leathers, giving priority to the materials traditionally used for small leather goods, such as cobra, lambskin or kidskin. He then tried out several potential lines for women, experimenting with new materials and original designs. With his keen interest in design, he perfected his creations, experimenting with novel outlines, shapes and volumes. Longchamp's real breakthrough in broadening its appeal to women was the introduction of the *LM* line of handbags, created from brown and beige embossed leather. Thanks to this collection, the company won over a substantial Japanese clientele as early as the 1970s. At that time, few luxury brands exported their creations to Japan. The *LM* collection came to represent the perfect embodiment of elegance *à la française*. In Europe, it was the introduction of drummed calfskin in 1980 that appealed to women. Its soft, sensual natural grain soon became inseparable from the brand's image. One of these bags could even be seen on the cover of *Paris Match*, dangling nonchalantly from the arm of Princess Caroline of Monaco.

It was Uncle Alain, ever-faithful to the company, who supplied Longchamp with this incredible leather via his frequent expeditions to Argentina and Uruguay. Lizard and crocodile were also used in all shapes and sizes, along with supple, silky lambskin and gentle sealskin. Philippe's creative impulse had pushed the search for the perfect material to the limit.

As well as things seemed to be going, a new misfortune was just around the corner. Consumed by grief since the death of her husband, Madame Cassegrain passed away in 1980. Philippe became Longchamp's chairman. Jean-François supported him for several more years, but he was already looking elsewhere. Dreaming of new adventures, he discretely withdrew from the business in 1987, to pursue his own interests.

Below: Catalog page showing the nylon
and calfskin luggage collection.

Opposite: The first series of photographer's Ken Griffith's
advertising campaigns inspired by equestrian themes, 1984.

Opposite: Advertising campaign, 1987.
Rachel Riley photographed by Daniel Jouanneau.

Below: Ken Griffith's advertising campaign, 1984.

Before this separation the pair drove Longchamp's creative development forward at a quick pace. That was when the brand's first flagship handbags appeared. The *Derby* collection was launched in 1982. Its bucket and pouch bags (*sac seau* and *cartouchière*) were an immediate, wide-spread success. The creations quickly appeared one after the other, each more original than the last, often based on the metaphor of "twisted" or redirected functionality. Advertising campaigns, which up until then had been rare, appeared more frequently in magazines. Beginning in 1984, Longchamp affirmed its place in the arts, drawing inspiration from the poetic and elegant equestrian world. Over the years, the feminine presence became more pronounced in these campaigns, hinting at the radical break that occurred several years later, when the company began to focus on the iconography of fashion and the image of women. Longchamp began to take on the allure of a true luxury brand, affirming its style at an ever-accelerating pace while developing a finer, more precise iconographic vocabulary.

A new generation of Cassegrains also began to take an interest in the company. Certain evenings, when Philippe came home from work in Segré, he found the whole family gathered together, impatiently awaiting his return. As soon as he had crossed the threshold, his children – Sophie, Jean and Olivier –, surrounded him, hopping up and down in delight, looking for the bag of prototypes hidden behind his back. The family home resounded with the children's laughter. Philippe's wife shared these moments of intimacy and closeness with them without, however, participating officially in the development of the company. That would come soon enough. Michèle Cassegrain had always worked in the gourmet meats industry. She adored her career, but the hours required by her work clashed with those of the rest of the family. When the idea of moving on to something else briefly crossed her mind, Philippe jumped at the opportunity to suggest that she join the Longchamp "stable".

Several weeks later Michèle Cassegrain accepted Philippe's suggestion and opened her first boutique in Paris's fashionable sixteenth arrondissement. That was Paris's first Longchamp boutique exclusively dedicated to Longchamp products. The experiment was a success. Michèle quickly got caught up in the game and longed to open a shop on the Rue Saint-Honoré, which, for her, represented the "life blood" of Paris. The Cassegrains discovered a promising location at number 390 of the famous street. The negotiations seemed to go on without end, but finally on July 5, 1988, Longchamp inaugurated its first flagship store. The store, designed by the decorator Patrice Nourissat, featured natural materials, ranging from leather to light-stained wood. It was from this new "flagship" that the network of stores dedicated exclusively to Longchamp products began to spread throughout the world.

A heartwarming story of abiding love

The strength of the feelings shared by Jean and Renée Cassegrain for each another left a profound mark on their family and friends. The sudden disappearance of her husband inflicted a mortal wound on Madame Cassegrain. Her son Dominique sheds some light:

"Behind every man, there is almost always a woman. In the Cassegrain family, the men commanded the front of the stage, but their success would have been meaningless without the unconditional support of their wives and children. That was true for Jean and Renée, and it is still true today for Philippe and his wife Michèle. When my father died, my mother decided that she would not survive him. She even instructed that any mail not addressed to "Madame Jean Cassegrain" be returned to the sender. Longchamp is much more than a business. It is also a legendary love story – the story of our parents."

Below: Jean Cassegrain as a child, 1969.

Opposite: The façade of the first Longchamp boutique in Paris, at 390 rue Saint-Honoré.

Memories of Longchamp...
By Michèle Cassegrain

"Longchamp has always been a part of our daily lives. In the days when the exhibitions were held at the Porte de Versailles, Monsieur Cassegrain even asked me to bring the children, who were still babies. Even though I wasn't born into the leather goods business, I have the feeling that it has always been a part of me.

The opening of our first boutique on Saint-Honoré in 1988 was an important step for Longchamp. The boutiques quickly opened one after the other all throughout Europe. Thanks to the talent and energy of those who helped me expand, we were able to maintain our forward momentum. It was a pleasure working with those who helped begin this adventure."

Jean-François Cassegrain, talent scout

"One day I went to the Leather Exhibition, without much conviction. I couldn't find anything I liked. Around 6 p.m., exhausted, I started to walk up the aisle on my way back to the car. I was a little grumpy, but whistling a tune to cheer myself up. Suddenly, a young man called out to me: "Hey, you're a not a bad whistler!" Continuing without a pause: "Did you visit my stand?" Naturally, I had not. "What do you sell?" I ventured somewhat sheepishly. The young man then took me back to his stand and held up two incredibly soft black leather skins. It was drummed calfskin – a leather we later consumed in huge quantities – in millions of square feet.

Some time later, as I was on my way back to Longchamp, I came across one of our suppliers in the street, who looked crestfallen. He hadn't been able to make an appointment to present his new product. I led him into my office so he could show me his samples. And there, he took out a magnificent swatch of coated fabric. I fell in love with it immediately. This was the legendary cloth that we used for our leather-trimmed *Derby* collection – which was an overwhelming success for at least six years! The bags came in black, brown, white and navy, and our customers adored them!"

Jean-François Cassegrain during a visit to Hong Kong in 1979, in front of an assortment of *LM* handbags crafted from *Shadow* printed leather.

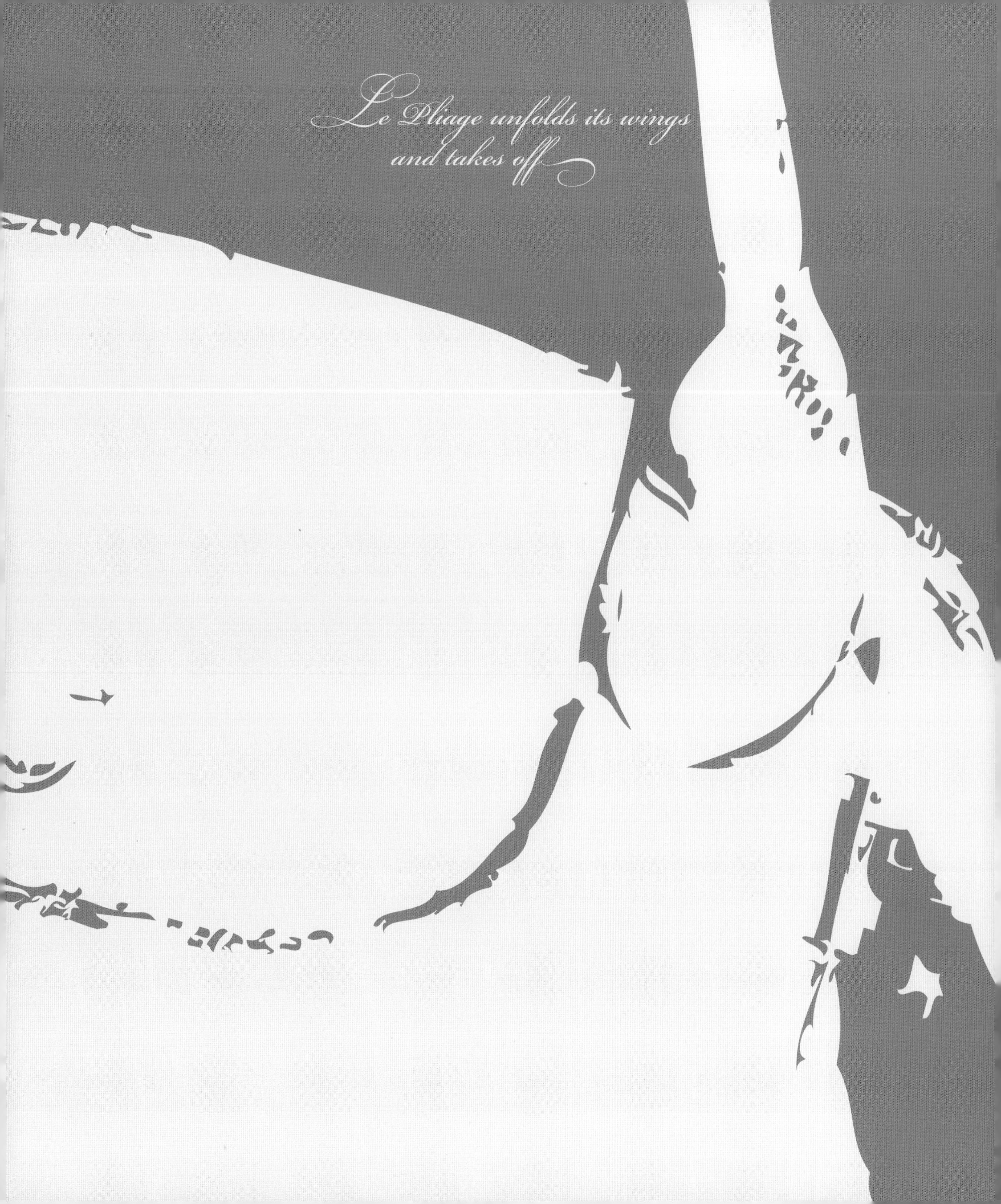
Le Pliage unfolds its wings
and takes off

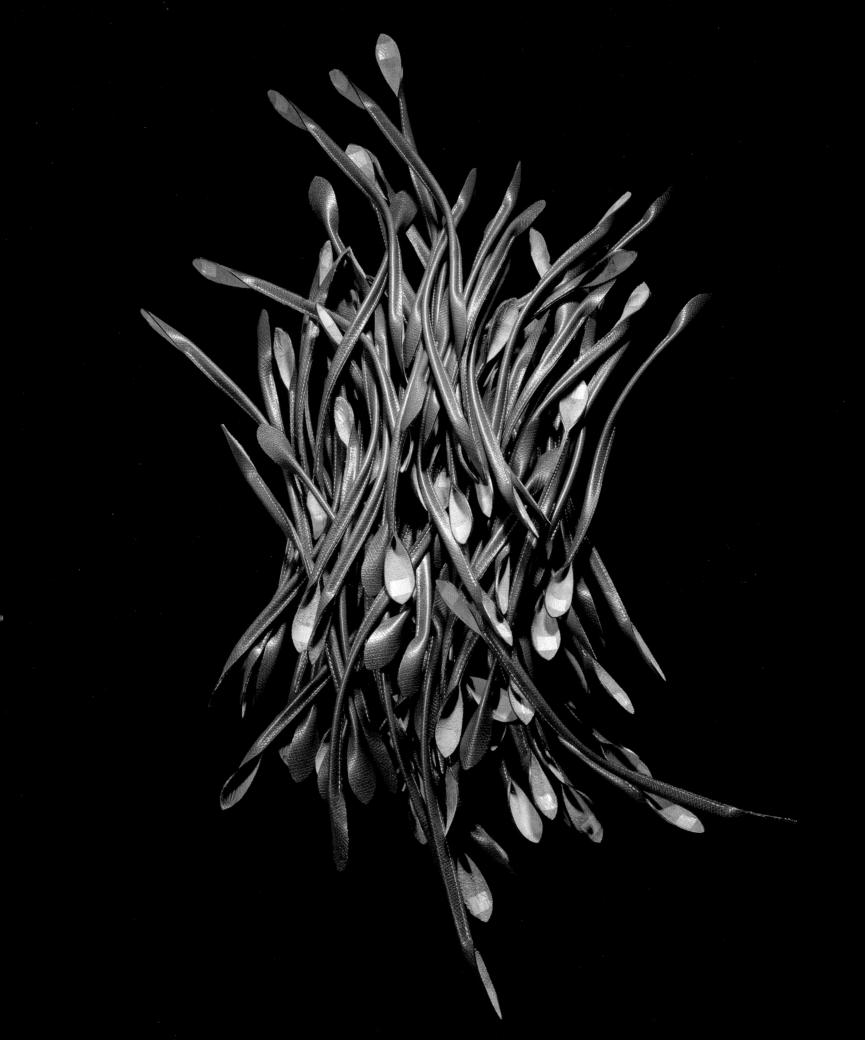

No introduction required. *Le Pliage* is to Longchamp what the *madeleine* is to Proust…
A symbol.
A phenomenon!
Above all, an ambassador, with over 12 million sold throughout the world.

Yet there was nothing to suggest the extent of the success. When Philippe Cassegrain developed *Le Pliage* in 1993, the appeal of light tote bags for the chic set was not a new phenomenon. Indeed, lightness has always been a puzzle for any respectable leather goods manufacturer. How do you balance feather-light weight with sturdiness in a functional bag? The equation seemed unsolvable. Riddles such as these naturally aroused the curiosity of the Cassegrain clan – and of Philippe, in particular, who stubbornly set out to solve the enigma. In fact, he had never stopped working on this impossible accessory since the start of his career at the company. At the beginning of the 1970s, he even designed a very promising prototype created from khaki nylon. The discovery of this material was nearly by accident: a former fellow leather goods producer, who subsequently sold coated nylon to the French army, offered to sell him a supply of irregular fabric. This product, intended for the manufacture of military groundsheet, had nothing *irregular* about it except the name: in reality, the smallest snag condemned vast quantities of otherwise flawless material. Philippe jumped at the opportunity. The nylon was splendid. Trimmed with pigskin leather, its beauty was enhanced without appreciably increasing its weight. Eureka! He had found the perfect solution. Longchamp produced a whole line using this new material. It was indeed a revolutionary material in the world of fine leather goods. Faced with bags that were either too heavy or too fragile, Longchamp created its own revolution in luggage departments: toiletry cases, garment bags, carry-on bags, tennis bags and so on. The polymorphous nature of the material lent itself to a multitude of uses such as the *Loch Ness*, a flat nylon "pancake" that magically transformed into a travel bag by simply pulling on a zipper.
For the first time, lambskin was combined with engineered fabric. Christened the *Lunar* collection, this ethereal line established a firm foothold at Longchamp prior to the addition of a line of black canvas bags trimmed with gold leather, dubbed the *Black Moon* collection.

Preceding page: A cluster of Russian leather handles for use on *Pliage* bags.

Below: A catalog page showing a range of nylon luggage trimmed with calfskin.

Opposite: First advertising campaign for the *Pliage* bag, 1995.

NYLON GARNI CUIR   LONGCHAMP

Memories of Longchamp...
By Philippe Cassegrain

"During a trip to the US, I took a prototype for a collapsible travel bag. The bag was supposed to be practical, but using it turned out to be much too complicated. This only made me want to create a new version that would be much lighter and much easier to use.

The result of this experimentation was the *Xtra-bag*, which is made of a single piece of fabric that's one of my father's particular favorites. The fabric I selected was nylon, a strong yet light material that nobody had previously used for bags. The bag was sold folded in its carrying bag, which meant that it could be easily stowed in a suitcase for later use, so you can see why I called it the *Xtra-bag*.

In 1993, I reworked the idea to create *Le Pliage*. More playful and modern yet in the spirit of the *Xtra-bag*, the *Pliage* is available in many colors, many of which are new every season. Its simple chic style will never go out of fashion."

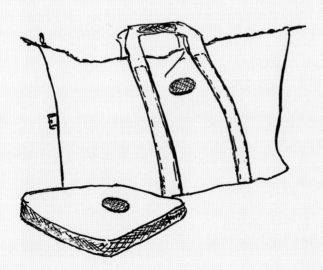

Opposite: Sketch for the *Xtra-Bag* and its case drawn by Philippe Cassegrain.

Below: A color wheel of *Pliage* bags.

Philippe continued his quest for the ideal shape. His next invention was the *Xtra-Bag*, a "back-up bag," that could be folded up and slipped into a small carrying case, ready for use whenever needed. This forerunner of the *Pliage* line already had the characteristic shape so well-known today, but it didn't yet have a flap or snap fastener on the back.

This trial run, as convincing as it was, did not yet completely satisfy its creator. Philippe was obsessed with the idea for nearly twenty years – until the launch of the collection introduced in 1993, when the descendant of the *Xtra-Bag* finally defied the laws of gravity and blasted off on its way to orbit the globe. The famous *Le Pliage* tote bag was born. It was really quite simple – the hard part was coming up with the idea. The trapezoidal-shaped bag had to fulfill certain conditions to be admitted to the very select circle of genuine *Pliage* bags: in particular, it needed to be made of heavy nylon fabric, with a flap pocket, two gracefully curved handles and two small tanned Russian leather lugs, all tied together by a snap fastener on the back. The material can

be folded and unfolded with a quick slight of hand, like origami into a square the size of a pocket book as light as a feather.

From the very beginning, Philippe had ambitious plans for this newcomer. It was produced in several different sizes ranging from handbag to luggage size, and was available in a dozen different colors, half of which are new each season. As soon as it arrived in stores, the *Pliage* bag threw all preconceived ideas about style out the window. Young women were infatuated with it; so were their mothers and even their grandmothers. It was not long before men jumped on the bandwagon. One often ran across elegant gentlemen in train stations using a large *Pliage* bag as a travel bag. *Le Pliage* totes were also filled with diapers and baby bottles, computers or books and other gear for the beach. This legendary bag achieved success in every country of the world.

Encouraged by its popularity, Philippe didn't stop there, but created even more unusual shapes and experimented with novel new materials. The *Le Pliage* brothers were talked about everywhere for their daring innovations: they added transparent pockets, cut the bags from off-beat printed fabric, adopted exotic stylistic elements – nothing could stop their momentum. The minimalist lines of *Le Pliage* seemed to authorize every trick in the book. Like a white page, which becomes a fertile ground for the imagination, the bags' elegant curves readily lent themselves to all the innovations introduced by the company.

For Longchamp's fiftieth anniversary, well-known master chef Alain Passard tried his hand at creating a chic shopping bag version of *Le Pliage*, designed to make the rounds of gourmet markets. This version was taller and equipped with a rigid drawer-compartment to separate the provisions and elegantly protect the strawberries from the leg of lamb. The most recent version, however, drew on the inventive narrative style of Dutch graphic designer Robert Wagt. He sketched out a minimalist portrayal of a day in a woman's life right on the fabric. The design was then embroidered on the material so that it appeared to be an impromptu sketch. To make sure the outlines traced by the thread were as graceful as those of a charcoal pencil, Longchamp didn't hesitate to go to great lengths. Their philosophy was to create a new tool for each new challenge. "Each impossible project incites us to re-invent our know-how," they continually stress at Longchamp. The technical means used to faithfully reproduce the drawings of Robert Wagt came close to the precision of the Swiss watchmaker's art. Perfection does not tolerate vague approximation. After forty-five minutes of embroidery, the fabric is finally turned into a bag. And a new *Pliage* is born.

Opposite: The *Pliage* bag designed by master chef Alain Passard for the fiftieth anniversary of Longchamp. Basil green nylon trimmed with Russian leather and drawer bottom.

Following page: Dimitri Tolstoï's advertising campaign, in 2000, showing the nylon *Pliage* and its canvas embroidered version.

CHAQUE SAISON,
LE PLIAGE LONGCHAMP EST L'ESPÈCE
LA PLUS CONVOITÉE.

CÉLADON

MÉSANGE

PAMPLEMOUSSE

CITRON VERT

LONGCHA

PARIS

The same approach was used for each new creation. The American designer Jeremy Scott had always been particularly fond of the flights of fancy of this universal bag. When he, in turn was invited to express himself on the canvas, he created the limited-edition (100 copies) *Le Pliage Poodle*, adorned with a purple poodle. The designer has also just created *Stomp*, a bag printed with a trail of footprints, and *Gold Card*, the *Pliage* tote that makes bankers nervous – in his tongue-in-cheek designs, luxury icons are re-imagined to create a whole new style.

It was inevitable in today's digital era that Longchamp would also infuse that virtual energy into its celebrated bag. Since 2003, the *Le Pliage* line can be ordered on the internet and lends itself perfectly to the light-hearted game in which each customer designs his or her own bag. The bag is fully customizable, from the length of the handles, the color combination, the finish of the accessories, the marking on the flap, all the way to the calligraphy and colors of the personal message to be embroidered on the bag.

In the workshops in Segré, each piece is produced with infinite patience, faithfully reproducing the "sweet nothings" devised by countless virtual lovebirds for each other. But the sweetest message of all is the one engraved in the hearts of Longchamp's employees: "I love you to distraction – for a long, long… Longchamp… uh… long time".

Le Pliage...

By Luc Fremont, Industrial Director of the Longchamp workshops

"Philippe Cassegrain had these bags shut away in a corner of his office for some time. I didn't like them at all. I found them too simple. But when we launched the orders, the start-up was phenomenal! We even had to reorganize our workshops around this bag. It forced us to make some big leaps forward in terms of production."

Le Pliage...

By Michèle Cassegrain

"*Le Pliage* arrived in shops in December 1993. I can only say one thing: it was extraordinary! It was not yet in the window display, but people asked for it all the same. Without advertising or publicity of any kind, this bag was an immediate success. It marked the history of our company for ever."

Opposite: Daniel Aron's advertising campaign for the transparent *Pliage*, in 1998, created by Sophie Delafontaine.

Following pages: Creative variations on the *Pliage*.
A *Pliage* sampler.

Le Pliage...
By Sophie Delafontaine

"One day, I suggested that we make a transparent *Pliage*. My father and brother were dubious. So they challenged me to a dare: "If you agree to put your personal affairs in a transparent bag and show everybody what you have inside for eight days, we will add it to the collection." Of course I took them up on it.

So we produced a transparent version of *Le Pliage*, with an advertisement featuring a photo of a bag filled with water, transformed into a goldfish bowl. It was a very poetic photo. I think it made a profound impression on the public."

Tracey Emin 2005

Chine 2007

Pensées Cristal 2000

Les Créations 2000

Cristal Logo 2005

Russe 2007

Western 2006

Japon 2007

Garden 2006

Western 2006

Babies 2006

Teddy Bear 2003

Wallpaper 2002

Smoking 2002

Curiosity 2006

Black Déco 2004

Flanelles Brodées 1999

Les Sports 1998

Pliage Cuivre 2001

Pliage Cuivre 2001

Kyoto 2002

Exotic 2003

Biarritz 2002

Pliage Les Créations 2000

Poetic 2003

Millefiori 2005

Plume d'Argent 2004

Pliage Club 2007

Funny P 2001

Patch 2001

Fou du roi 2003

Pliage Les Créations 2000

Arc-en-ciel 2005

Frivole 2006
Dominique Cassegrain's creation.

Le Pliage by Longchamp: a convergence of opposites

Elyette Roux, a sociologist specializing in the world of luxury and a university professor (Université Paul Cézanne Aix-Marseille III, CERGAM-IAE Aix-en-Provence), analyzes the universality of the *Pliage* bag and attempts to solve its enigma.

Together with Gilles Lipovetsky, Elyette Roux co-authored *Le luxe éternel, de l'âge du sacré au temps des marques* (Gallimard, Paris, 2003).

"I was monitoring an exam in my classroom at the IAE School of Management in Aix-en-Provence, when I started to notice the satchels and handbags of my female students – one, two, three, four, five Longchamp *Pliage* bags! That was a lot for a class of forty students!

And it naturally got me thinking: how is it that these girls still prefer *Pliage* bookbags or handbags, which were already popular with their mothers' generation – and mine. How does this brand succeed in attracting followers from one generation to the next?

To understand these students' attraction to the brand, I asked them to write a short narrative description of what Longchamp represented for them. I then used semiotic analysis to compare these narratives with major consumer values: use values vs. basic values. These values were brought to the fore by the semiotician Jean-Marie Floch whose research was based on the work of Greimas on objects of value.

Use values are primarily utilitarian or functional in nature; they refer to a practical valuation of the object: in this case, Longchamp's *Pliage* bags. When the object is endowed with *basic* values, that means, on the contrary, that it refers to the basic identity of their owners, their status and social or professional position. It therefore meets *basic* or so-called *existential* values. Theoretically, use values and basic values are considered to be opposites, but the reality of postmodern individuals implies a convergence of opposites. Use values (simplicity and practicality, in the case of Longchamp) must be satisfied in the same way as basic values: it is this convergence which makes up the identity of a modern young woman: "active, mobile, open-minded, envied by the whole world", to quote the words of one of my students.

When *Le Pliage* is analyzed through the prism of the semiotic square, one immediately notes that this bag corresponds to the paradoxical converging of opposites sought by the contemporary female consumer.

If we continue the decomposition of the consumer values which the brand generates as it is experienced by our young students, two other

Consumer values related to Longchamp (semiotic square)

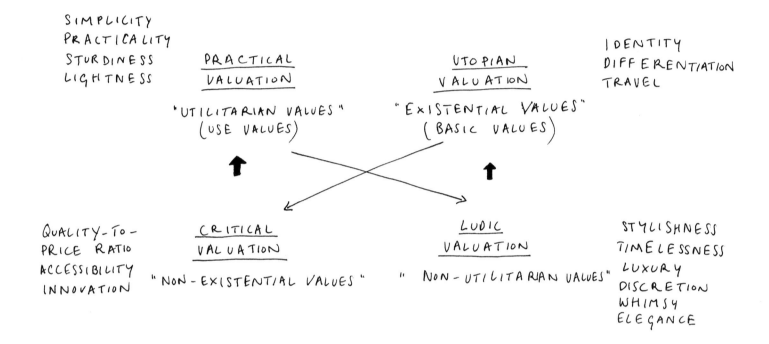

SIMPLICITY
PRACTICALITY
STURDINESS
LIGHTNESS

PRACTICAL
VALUATION

"UTILITARIAN VALUES"
(USE VALUES)

UTOPIAN
VALUATION

"EXISTENTIAL VALUES"
(BASIC VALUES)

IDENTITY
DIFFERENTIATION
TRAVEL

QUALITY-TO-
PRICE RATIO
ACCESSIBILITY
INNOVATION

CRITICAL
VALUATION

"NON-EXISTENTIAL VALUES"

LUDIC
VALUATION

"NON-UTILITARIAN VALUES"

STYLISHNESS
TIMELESSNESS
LUXURY
DISCRETION
WHIMSY
ELEGANCE

categories of values of the semiotic square are also reflected. For *ludic* values, which fall into the category of non-utilitarian values, the students cite stylishness and timeless luxury, which are at one and the same time unobtrusive, elegant and whimsical. For *critical* values, the students mention the quality-to-price ratio, as well as the accessible and innovative aspects of the brand.

Longchamp's intergenerational success is thus based on a paradoxical convergence of contemporary consumer values, leading the "modern" mothers, like their "postmodern" daughters, to develop an attachment to the brand, and particularly to the *Pliage* bags, which satisfy all four consumer values."

[1] J. M. Floch, "J'aime, j'aime, j'aime... publicité automobile et système des valeurs de consommation", in *Sémiotique, Marketing et Communication: sous les signes, les stratégies*, Paris, PUF, 1990, p. 119-152.
[2] A.G. Greimas, "Un problème de sémiotique narrative: les objets de valeur", in *Du Sens II*, Paris, Seuil, 1983, p. 19-48.

Soaring technical virtuosity

Longchamp has a very well-guarded secret – an industrial strength so jealously preserved that it is rarely suspected. Ever since the Segré workshop opened in 1959, it has been enlarged on a regular basis, with additional facilities spreading out from this base throughout the Angers region. In 1969, Jean Cassegrain bought out a manufacturer in Rémalard, in the Orne. Then in 1972, he acquired the Ernée facility in the Mayenne. In the decade before 2000, three new units were added to this network: in Combrée (Maine-et-Loire), Château-Gontier (Mayenne) and Montournais (Vendée). The Segré facility itself was enlarged and modernized to meet increasing demand. The firm's workshops, infused with Longchamp know-how, have instilled their knowledge of the business into every nook and cranny of the operation.

This continually developing industrial network constitutes the technological foundation that enables Longchamp to simultaneously innovate, produce and deliver its creations to the entire world. In 1982, the Cassegrain family even decided to extend beyond the borders of France and set up a factory on the island of Mauritius, followed by a production partnership in China in 1997. In 2001, workshops in Morocco and Tunisia were added to increase Longchamp's industrial capacity, which has been managed for the last twenty years by the firm and experienced hand of Luc Fremont.

In these production "incubators," hidden away from curious eyes, skilled leather artisans debate ergonomics, devise foolproof handles and cut out leather strips the size of a postage stamp, all with meticulous attention to detail. The oldest production shop of them all, the Segré facility, now opens its doors for a one-of-a-kind tour, with a running commentary by some of its central figures. Without them, Longchamp's legendary know-how would not be what it is today.
The employees of Segré have agreed to share some of their most personal memories, professional secrets and demonstrations of talent.

It all begins in the Models and Methods workshop, managed by the master artisans of volume and surface rendering. They frequently receive highly imaginative sketches of bags based on unrealizable concepts, along with perplexing diagrams they must decipher. The model makers transform the drawing into a prototype entirely by hand. The dizzying array of instruments scattered across their tables, including metal or horn folding sticks, awls, molds, glues, brushes, is what makes this technically wizardry possible. Even though much is done by hand, the modeling process is computerized to ensure the final pattern is surgically precise.
The model is worked and reworked until perfection is achieved. The resulting pattern will be used to draw up the assembly cards and launch the production of the metal dies used to cut the materials.

Preceding page: *Maxi-Rival* bag crafted from orange crocodile leather.
A special edition limited to three bags, 2007.

Opposite: The shop workers pose in front of the first Segré factory, constructed in 1959.
Below: Aerial view of the second Segré factory, which was enlarged in 1997.

Following pages: Spools of multicolored thread and a chromatic range of leather labels for use inside the bags.

Émilie Chavet-Pinçon has been a model maker at Longchamp for eight years.

"I came to Longchamp from the world of high fashion, and had to learn the hard way what "Made in Longchamp" means. In fact, it can be summed up in two concepts: attention to detail and hard work.

Out of the hundreds of new models designed for each collection, we always have at least one real brain-teaser, something practically impossible to produce – which we finally resolve by sheer patience and perseverance, no matter how long it takes!

Occasionally we receive orders for crocodile bags. Since this is not a product that can be mass-produced, I often take charge of the order and produce these articles one by one. There is a whole art to creating products from crocodile leather, in addition to the intense pressure: it is impossible to ignore the outrageous value of the material I have in my hands. There's no room for error."

Above, left to right: Embossing irons used to imprint the Longchamp logo.
Placement of a cutting die on a white patent leather skin.
Lumière Tropicale fabric, Spring-Summer 2008.
Meticulous over-stitching of a drummed calfskin bag.

Nadine Certenais works in the Models shop and has 33 years of experience with the company.

"My greatest pleasure is working with extremely high-quality materials. The work is very meticulous, and that's what I like about it."

The lines dictate the style. Detailing is the signature of luxury. Short cuts are impossible. Whether the detail in question concerns the relief of the logo or the tint of the ultimate finishing touches, each square inch of a bag in production requires the most fastidious attention. To find solutions for unsolvable questions, a team of experts from the Methods and Models department steps in. Their credo: any difficulty can be overcome with the right approach…

Michel Pendans, who has been with the company for 37 years, is Longchamp's Development manager.

"My work consists of managing part of the production, from the skin to final

Opposite: Black patent leather *Légende* bag.

Following pages: Stitching of handle chapes
on a metallized leather *Cosmos* bag.
Turning in of a front-piece design using a bone folding stick.

assembly. I look for technical solutions in response to the requirements of the creative process. For example, when the logo changes I need to modify our way of producing it. I always look for the subtlest way of embossing the leather in order to maintain the streamlined silhouette of the horse.

Longchamp products can be differentiated from others by the quality of their finish. For the *Légende* bag, we had to design a special method of finishing the edges of the leather used for the label. We conducted countless experiments to come up with the solution: a sable-hair brush to apply the color to such a narrow surface."

Without bags, there would be no need for leather…, but most importantly, without leather, there would be no bags at all… The department responsible for the inspection of materials applies meticulous attention to each skin received. Equipped with a thickness gauge, an inspector of this crucial department scrutinizes up to 1,600,000 square feet of leather each year with an expert eye. Leathers from all over the world, from Brazil to Uruguay, and closer to home, from France and Italy are subjected to their scrutiny. They check each skin one by one in accordance with the quality criteria established by the company, comparing colors and evaluating the leather's "hand" or feel. Large models require a perfect skin, while it is possible to work around flaws for smaller models. When you consider that each bag requires from 5 to 8 square feet of leather, you can imagine the scope of their job.

Jean-Charles Gagneux, the facility's Leather Warehousing manager, has been with Longchamp for five years.

"You can't cut corners with leather. Relying on vague approximations is out of the question. We never relax our vigilance concerning the choice of materials; quality always takes priority over quantity.

We have an invaluable treasure in our archives: a two-hundred-year-old skin. It was part of a batch of skins found on shipwrecked boat two centuries ago. You can imagine how we feel when we touch such exceptional skins! In fact, we use a replica of this leather for the *Pliage* line."

The "Russian leather" used for Le Pliage *takes its name from a batch of skins found during the 1980s on board the* Frau Metta Catharina, *a ship that sailed from St. Petersburg in 1786, and sunk off the coast of Plymouth in Cornwall. Its highly unusual diamond-shaped grain inspired Philippe Cassegrain when he created the legendary* Le Pliage *bag. He was enchanted by the weathered look of the material and its distressed patina with its Slavic connotations, set off by the juxtaposition of the leather with the bag's shimmering nylon fabric. (Author's note)*

When the various metal dies have cut the various components of a bag to be assembled are finally ready, the leather craftsmen can begin putting the pieces of the puzzle together. They must be able to work around the minor flaws in the material and the randomly shaped outlines of the skins. Full-grain leather, with its rich veining, requires a great deal of time and concentration, as does drummed calfskin, which is only entrusted to the most experienced artisans.

Christine Garnier is manager of the Cloth Cutting shop and has been employed at Longchamp for 31 years.

"Like many people here, my first job was in the Small Leather Goods shop. The work is very manually demanding, and requires a high degree of precision. Then I discovered cutting, with lining material. When *Le Pliage* was introduced, we created a team entirely devoted to "fabric cutting".

It is interesting to observe the changes in our production tools over the last thirty years. In the past, we cut out the components one by one with a leather knife. The garment bags were cut with an electric chisel and all the holes were punched by hand, using a mallet. That is what you call real hand cutting! Even though the tools are more sophisticated today, it is still important not to lose manual dexterity.

A good leather cutter needs about two years of training. You need to acquire a feeling for the skin right away. For cloth, it's a little different. The cutter doesn't need to search for the proper placement. On the other hand, the cloth cutter needs to respect the direction of the warp and weft. A single bag includes a dozen different components, including the reinforcements."

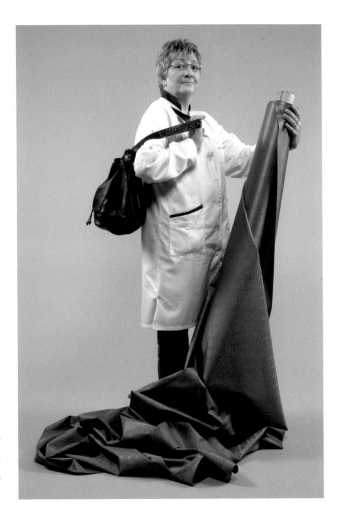

Once the cloth and leather panels have been cut, the bag can be assembled. Each workshop assembles its bags from A to Z, from the zippers to the color finishes on the edges. Longchamp feels strongly that the workshops producing its creations must be versatile. Dividing up the assembly of a bag between several different teams is not an option. Each shop is responsible for its own production. This emphasis on versatility makes it possible to integrate a wide range of different activities within the same shop, particularly such functions as table activities, preparation activities and stitching activities. Certain specializations have emerged on the fringes of these three main categories, such as the paring station and the tinting station (the latter operation is often accomplished with an artist's brush). The various areas of expertise complement and enrich each other, and are transmitted to colleagues at the same time. The craftswomen who work in these shops are motivated by one overriding concern: the desire to hand down the art of their dexterity to the next generation...

Opposite: Christine Garnier, manager of the Segré fabric cutting shop.

Following pages, left to right:
Luc Frémont, Industrial Director of the Segré plant.
Bruno Poirier, manager of the Methods and Models department, with his mother, who was one of the first employees of the Segré workshop. They are carrying a leather duffel bag and beggar's bag from the *LM* collection re-issued for the firm's sixtieth anniversary.
Laurent Marcassin, manager of the Models shop, behind the prototype for the tutu bag which he produced for Agnès Letestu during Longchamp's fiftieth anniversary.
Sewer Michèle Gastineau and the collection designed by the artist Tracey Emin in 2004.

Christiane Le Guilloux, who manages the Bag Assembly shop, has been with the firm for 31 years.
"When I started working for Longchamp, we were still making the leather-covered pipes. I also made cigarette cases, large lambskin garment bags and travel bags. Everything was done by hand. When Isabelle Guyon and Sophie Delafontaine joined the Style department, many things changed because they began to create very different models with Monsieur Philippe. The technical know-how remains the same.
It takes a long time to become a competent leather worker. Workers have their own ideas, their own way of doing things, their little secrets and so on. Some pieces require several hours of work, and not necessarily those you might expect.
I am naturally very proud of what we do, and even prouder when I see our products in stores. Each day is different; we really enjoy ourselves. The *Vintage* handbag was a real source of satisfaction. And the *Légende* speaks for itself!"

Michèle Gastineau works in the Assembly shop as a bag sewer and has been with Longchamp for 25 years.
"I began my career at Longchamp in the Small Leather Goods shop, where I was responsible for binding. Nobody knows just how complicated binding is. You need to constantly search for little tricks to make sure that the material is always absolutely perfect.
I was the one who stitched artist Tracey Emin's luggage! I'll never forgot as long as I live! You should come back and watch us stitch rabbit: we have to shear off the edges of the fur in order to sew the leather. There are little hairs all over the place; we are all wrapped up in our aprons and must wear masks to make sure we can breathe!"

All articles meant to be slipped into a pocket or bag are considered small leather goods. At Longchamp, the expertise of the Small Leather Goods workshops merits a high-quality label. It takes five years of experience to gain proficiency in assembling a small leather article from beginning to end. Very few have what it takes to complete the training for millimeter-accurate precision, where the sole criterion for success is the eye's expertise and fingers' agility.

Madeleine Duveau works in the Small Leather Goods shop and has 37 years of hands-on experience.
"The first time I stepped into a workshop was on September 1st, 1970. I was 16 at the time. The old timers taught me everything. We were

working eight at a table, and the woman with the most experience taught us all the tricks of the trade.

Most small leather articles are time consuming to produce. When they are cut from complicated leathers, it takes even longer. Elephant leather slackens, and the grain of ostrich leather squeaks when you insert the needle, but the leathers I've worked with most often are probably lizard and crocodile. The price of the material is set to less than half an inch, so it's best to avoid errors. One thing is certain: the "hand" of the leather has changed considerably. In the past, I worked with very stiff, rigid leathers. Today, the line of leathers used is much less rigid; more supple leathers are preferred."

The bag is now ready to leave the workshops. The company's international prestige and worldwide distribution network require an efficient Shipping department. Far from considering this department an entity of secondary importance, Longchamp has put the accent on modernizing its logistics tools so that the raspberry *Le Pliage* coveted by the young woman from Shanghai will reach her as quickly as the glacé leather *Légende* ordered by the elegant New Yorker.

Bruno Poirier is the manager of the Methods and Models department, and has worked for Longchamp for 23 years.
"I have always had a good knowledge of the company – after all, my mother was part of Longchamp's first production unit –, so the workshops held few secrets for me."

Laurent Marcassin is manager of the Models shop and has been with Longchamp for 17 years.
"I will never forget the tutu bag I produced for Agnès Letestu, the prima ballerina. It was the largest bag I ever made. It was an imposing challenge; the main requirement was that the tutu could not be folded. I had to constantly rework the sketches, while respecting the wishes of the artist. The result was truly marvelous…"

Luc Fremont has been Longchamp's industrial director for 20 years.
"Longchamp's strength? To have had the foresight to switch its core activities several times during its existence. Where other firms simply decline to the point of collapse, Longchamp was forward thinking enough to change with the times. Since it is a family affair, we have the privilege of interacting directly with the Cassegrain family. Decisions are made very rapidly, which helps everyone to work more productively."

Assortment of small leather articles.

Fashion takes the reigns

Memories of Longchamp…
By Jean Cassegrain, Longchamp CEO

"With each new generation of Cassegrains that joins into the venture, the commitment has held firm. Frankly, I never had any doubts; Longchamp always seemed like the obvious choice for me. I never really considered anything else. I had been going to trade shows abroad with my father for a long time, and everything fell into place quite naturally. But before joining, I chose to build up my experience elsewhere, in order to offer the company a true source of added value. I finally had the opportunity to join Longchamp. It was very exciting to have the opportunity to help extend the brand throughout the world. By opening stores in the US, Europe and Asia, Longchamp has been able to strengthen its foundation. Many challenges remain, but I'm confident that the next generation will passionately go about finding solutions to them."

Preceding page: Tan *Cosmos* bag.

Opposite: Front of the Longchamp boutique
in the Ginza district of Tokyo in May 2008.

Below: Multicolored bracelets from
the 2008 Spring-Summer collection.

Longchamp marked out its territory as a leader in women's handbags. The jockey and its tireless mount struck a note with women of the 1980s. In addition to being fastidious, women refused to be weighed down by a beggar's bag devoid of functionality. These elegant women refused to forgive fashion faux pas and excessively nostalgic clichés. Philippe Cassegrain understood them well. Their handbags must be forward-looking, bold without overdoing it, and charming without being excessively sentimental.

In a word, their bags must be "fashionable." Even though textile creations were beginning to arouse curiosity, the term was not yet taken for granted. This approach was not yet considered an assurance of success. Longchamp felt close affinities with the fashion world, however, and didn't hesitate to adopt its rarely used lexicon. When Philippe Cassegrain's son, Jean, began working at his side in 1991, he confirmed this strategic orientation. The company also strengthened its team in charge of design. In 1989, Philippe Cassegrain took on an invaluable assistant, Isabelle Guyon, a designer whose outsider's view of the enterprise helped the brand push its creativity to the limits.

Then, with the benefit of her previous experience in children's apparel, Philippe's daughter, Sophie Delafontaine, joined the duo in 1993 as a designer. She brought with her the tried and true working methods of the ready-to-wear industry, such as the organization of collections around overarching themes.

The decade of the 1990s justified Philippe Cassegrain's choices: the handbag irrepressibly continued its forward momentum towards new avenues of expression. This shift was undoubtedly the result of women's changing relationship with their handbags. They now felt that clothing should be coordina-

ted with their accessories. So little by little, the handbag became an integral part of their identity, a veritable coat of arms, which drew all eyes and transformed the woman carrying it.

In 1993, Isabelle Guyon created the *Roseau*, a large leather carry-all bag with a clasp in the form of a piece of bamboo. This bag marked the beginning of a succession of resounding successes, and quickly became the darling of journalists and trendy young women, marching on to conquer the hearts of young women all over the world. The *Roseau* was shown in advertisements, slung at the feet of fashion writers in the first row in front of the runway. At first glance, however, the bag looked like a real outsider: the Longchamp sales teams could hardly believe their eyes – a bag that couldn't even be worn over

Below: For its first advertising campaign, the *Roseau* bag, photographed by Daniel Aron in 1997, is seen in a front row seat of a fashion show.

Opposite: Black lacquered *Roseau* bag.

Following pages: Longchamp ready-to-wear: tweed coat and *Cult* bag made from lamb fur and black patent leather, Fall-Winter 2008-2009. Anorak with a lamb's fur collar and a leather *Légende* clutch bag, Fall-Winter 2008-2009.

the shoulder or properly closed. Certain dissenters voiced their concern: "It's sheer madness, Monsieur Philippe! It doesn't even keep the rain out!" But this kind of argument tended to have the opposite of effect on the Cassegrains – stubbornness runs in the family. When all was said and done, it turned out to be a stroke of genius, becoming an instant "best seller," a term that would soon be taken for granted at the firm.

In 2006, heading in the opposite direction of ready-to-wear brands, which were beginning to create handbags and luggage, Longchamp decided to broaden the scope of its activities to include women's clothing. But at Longchamp, apparel was listed in the collections as an "accessory." In addition to belts, gloves, scarves and jewelry, which the company had developed since the 1990s, it decided to offer a ready-to-wear line designed to accessorize its bags. Under the direction of Sophie Delafontaine, the company's emblematic detailing, such as adjustable tabs and rivets, found new use on materials borrowed from the leather goods industry, such as reverse shearling, nylon and lambskin.

Since the 1990s, the brand's collections had taken on a lighter image, featuring touches of color and a certain freshness. Taking the trend one step further, Jean and Sophie decided to show off their creations with a hint of glamour. The company called upon the well-known fashion photographer Andrea Klarin to produce its advertising campaign in 2002. It then turned to photographer Miles Aldridge for the 2005 campaign. English model, Lily Cole, lounging on the edge of a swimming pool, dominated the photo with her immense eyes and deadly charm. Her red mane, doll's face and smoldering presence soon lit up fashion shows all around the world. But Longchamp had spotted her first. Another scorching beauty, Kate Moss, joined the audacious crew in 2006, when she was under heavy fire from the media. Though the choice of the Cassegrain family seemed impudent to some, the family trusted her. For them, nothing counted but talent. The photos shot by Mario Sorrenti spotlighted the brand's new flagship bags. The first was the *Rival* in 2006. In 2007, it was the *Légende*'s turn in the limelight, toted by twig-like super model, Kate Moss, alias the "*Brindille*." And 2008 stands out for the meteoric ascent of the *Cosmos*, caught in the crossfire of photography's star duo, Mert Alas and Marcus Piggott.

These were trendsetting bags, representing the ultimate in elegance and style that were quickly adopted by celebrities: unauthorized photos of Madonna, Claudia Schiffer and Kate Moss confirmed that they had wholeheartedly welcomed Longchamp into their lives, thus consecrating the brand's widespread acceptance in the fashion world.

Below: Variations on belts.

Opposite: Fall-Winter 2002-2003 advertising campaign, photograph Andrea Klarin.

A question of angles…

By Xavier Auvillain, the advertising executive responsible for Longchamp's advertising campaigns

"Longchamp's advertising campaigns can be broadly grouped into three periods. In the 1980s, we developed the dreamlike world of horses, focusing on an equestrian style tinged with British accents. The company's luggage was associated with jockeys and stable-boys; while the stables called to mind the well-bred elegance of horse-riding.

But horses also evoked a somewhat masculine world, while Longchamp's creations aspired to appeal to women. As a result, we decided to move luggage into the background and focus the spotlight on the handbag, with a view to creating a closer link between the brand and the daily lives of women. Our advertisements began to include impromptu snapshots, which linked Longchamp with the everyday lives of young women, captured on the move. Gradually, a number of fashion brands began to develop their own leather accessories, establishing the idea that a handbag could be 'in fashion'… and then go 'out of fashion'. Longchamp responded to this offensive by proving that its products could also engage in "fashion-speak". The idea that handbags could be featured in seasonal collections gradually gained acceptance and our advertising campaigns followed suit. Longchamp's visual approach thus pushed femininity to the foreground, confirming the brand's move into the fashion world.

The question of whom to choose as the brand's ambassador then came up. We immediately ruled out the idea of a movie actress, since acting is not necessarily synonymous with fashion. The profession of fashion model, on the other hand, matched our expectations perfectly. A model is the very essence of the world of fashion. We still needed to find that unique person who would be the perfect fit, however. We didn't hesitate for long: Kate Moss was not just a fashion model, she was *the fashion model incarnate*, recognizable as a fashion icon from New York to Tokyo.

The photos were shot in New York by photographer Mario Sorrenti, and the public's reaction was very positive. So we decided to continue this collaborative effort, but we took a very different approach from one season to the next. For the 2008-09 autumn-winter campaign, Kate Moss posed for photographers Mert Alas and Marcus Piggott – together with a surprise guest star: the young actor Gaspard Ulliel. The setting was the Café de Flore, in Saint-Germain-des-Prés, since the ready-to-wear collection was inspired by Left Bank elegance.

It was an appropriate way for the brand to pay tribute to its roots: the city of Paris."

Preceding pages: Lily Cole photographed by Miles Aldridge, Spring-Summer 2005 advertising campaign.

Opposite: Kate Moss photographed by Mario Sorrenti, Fall-Winter 2006-2007 advertising campaign.

LONGCHAMP

PARIS

Longchamp's focus on equestrian imagery gradually fell into the background in the 1990s to make way for the fashion world. But the Cassegrains decided not to put the valiant horse out to pasture just yet: the little steed continued to lead the way like a lucky charm. Instead of doing away with it, Philippe redesigned it. The slightly clumsy outlines of the mount were re-sculpted to resemble a refined thoroughbred, as graceful as a shooting star. When the horse and rider galloped over leather, they were embossed, giving them a head start on their unbridled race. The racetrack itself was now crowed with 1,650 employees, compared to 300 in 1988, as the company's revenues quadrupled over ten years. This pace naturally encouraged the company to polish up its distribution network: its subsidiaries were strengthened via local commercial ties in countries such as Spain, South Korea, China and the United Kingdom. With nearly 2,000 multiple-brand retail outlets worldwide, the brand could henceforth boast of a presence in the world's most prestigious showcases, such as department stores in Tokyo's Ginza district or New York's Fifth Avenue.

The growing success of the Paris store on the rue Saint-Honoré prompted Michèle Cassegrain to move to number 404 of the same street. In this new, more expansive space she had the room she needed to display the brand's entire luggage line without feeling cramped. The new shop, also designed by Patrice Nourissat, opened on April 17, 1999. The international development of the Longchamp chain was not neglected: numerous new addresses were added to the list of shops, which increased in number from 35 in 1998, to over 100 in 2008.

The Longchamp bag proved to be an passionate globe-trotter.

Preceding pages: Kate Moss photographed by Mario Sorrenti, Spring-Summer 2008 advertising campaign.

Below: The front of the Longchamp boutique at 404 rue Saint-Honoré in Paris, in 2008.

Opposite: Photo for the magazine *Marie France*, in 2007. *Rival* bag.

Below: Photo for the German edition of *Glamour*, in 2008.

Tie and Dye tote bag, Spring 2008.

Following page: Astrakhan style *Cosmos* fur bag.

Memories of Longchamp...

By Sophie Delafontaine, Longchamp's artistic director

"We have always been immersed in the culture of Longchamp, first, by the simple fact that we all lived in the same building. I loved spending my free time in the Champs-Élysées store with my grandmother. The leather and cardboard smelled so good. I also spent a summer working in the Madison Avenue "Brigitte Cassegrain" shop in New York. It was an incredible experience for a 16-year-old girl!

My father had already created a little mini-handbag, just for me, when I was a little girl. When Longchamp began to expand its women's handbag collections, I was obviously very spoiled! I never had the same bag as everyone else. The bucket bag, for instance, was the envy of all the other girls at my school. I was always a step ahead of the crowd.
My father taught us to really love Longchamp products. As I grew up, he introduced me to various assembly methods and leathers – without ever lecturing me on what should or should not be done. I trained my eye all by myself, little by little, and developed my own critical faculties.

For many years, the firm relied on the equestrian metaphor to establish the quality of our *savoir-faire*. We emphasized elegance *à la française*, saddle-stitched leather, and a smart, sporty style. It was by capitalizing on this know-how that we were able to move our brand towards a more fashion-oriented approach. The sociological evolution of the handbag went hand in hand with our own thought processes. In the past, handbags played a purely functional role. A well-dressed woman had three bags: black, beige, and navy, which she kept for ten years. Today, women flit about from bag to bag, coordinating them with their outfits or the day's weather forecast. The bag has become a fashion accessory. And Longchamp has adapted its product line to reflect this new view."

New York, New York, 132, Spring Street

New York, New York, 132, Spring Street

Preceding page: Staircase of the Maison Unique.

Opposite: The steel landscape linking the ground floor to the upper level.

La Maison Unique represents Longchamp's most spectacular store to date and its hundredth worldwide sales location. The brick and glass loft is nestled in ultra-fashionable SoHo, the ultimate trendy address and spawning ground for art galleries and miscellaneous creative endeavors. Once again, Longchamp dares to venture where least expected.

Who would have thought it possible? It turns out almost no one. The space was totally awesome, with incredible, almost infinite potential. But there was a stumbling block, which threatened to make it unusable as a retail setting: nearly all the space was concentrated above street level. And all the experts agree: it is a well-known fact that customers are reluctant to climb stairs. They prefer to circulate freely, obstacle-free, just as they would in the street. In short, everyone wants to be on the bottom floor. So, if one is to believe the canons of universal commerce, a store cannot succeed when most of the space is on an upper floor. To do so would be pure folly.

Talk about a challenge! Jean Cassegrain, who takes after his grandfather, was not one to be daunted. He decided to solicit the help of London designer Thomas Heatherwick, convinced that all that was needed to entice people upstairs, without carrying them up, was a clever sleight of hand. The talented Englishman expressed a few reservations, for the sake of form, but then immediately entered into the spirit of it all. On paper, his designs seemed to proclaim: "A unique setting demands a unique solution."

Heatherwick conceived of the space as an imaginary landscape, where the ground curves up to meet the sky. The sky, in return, descends down along the walls via a gigantic light well cut through the building's roof, bringing daylight deep into the store's interior, all the way to street level, catching the eye and kindling desire. This ethereal beam of light points the way upward almost supernaturally. Then all the sudden steps cascade before the surprised visitor's eyes: thirty broad ribbons, floating down from the upper level to the store entrance like a flowing mantle descending from the heavens. The material, 55 tons of hot-rolled steel, flows down like lava in successive curves and folds, delicately and peacefully. This installation, a dramatic topography for a temple of architecture, borders on high art. Time doesn't matter. It never mattered. Six months of construction were needed for the cascade of ribbons alone. Then balustrades fashioned from clear polycarbonate were draped along the staircase using techniques borrowed from the construction of aircraft windshields. To create these rippled transparent sheets, the manufacturer used a piece of equipment, similar to a giant toaster, into which the balustrade panels were placed, one by one. The heat softens the polycarbonate, which is deformed and twisted by gravity, creating a unique, almost lunar, relief effect.

Upstairs, the ash ceiling is split into strips, which curve down along the walls toward the floor like flexible strips of bark. The shelves were organically created from the same material, and the idea was carried over to the maple floor where the furnishings, sleek wooden slabs for the display of merchandise, seem to rise up from the wooden floor itself.

Heatherwick also had the foresight to add an additional floor on the roof for the brand's offices and wholesale showroom, surrounded by a plant-covered terrace. After 111,000 hours of labor, La Maison Unique finally opened its doors in May 2006. This astonishing and astoundingly chic address created quite a stir. Customers now waltz up from the ground floor to the second floor with a light heart and a spring in their step. And a host of luminaries didn't need much persuasion to come lend their brilliance to the inauguration of this temple of style. Among them were Uma Thurman, Susan Sarandon, Maggie Gyllenhaal, Lucy Liu, Eva Mendes, Isabella Rossellini, Jeremy Scott, Anouck Lepere and Mario Sorrenti, who reverently came to celebrate the fantastic grand opening.

A look behind the scenes with Thomas Heatherwick

"Jean called me to let me know that he had found a potential site for a new store in New York. I immediately asked him to send me some photos, which he did. The images revealed an surprising choice of building for a flagship store.

I called him right back to check I understood the project correctly and discussed the complexities of the site. I even queried whether he should sign right away... To which he cheerfully responded: "Too late! I signed this morning!"

The place was really staggering, but most of the space was upstairs, with a very narrow ground floor.

The experience of working on the project was fantastic and unconventional. Jean was very involved in the creative effort and wanted something unique, that didn't resemble the other Longchamp stores in any way. He attended all the meetings in New York and was thoughtful and well considered. We suggested the addition of another level, to be used as a showroom, and the Cassegrain family agreed immediately and the move allowed us to increase the store's size by 50%. The key challenge next was to obtain permits from the New York authorities and find a talented contractor team able to deliver such an unusual scheme.

Above: Opening ceremony for the Maison Unique in May 2006.
Left to right: Uma Thurman and Dominique Cassegrain;
Susan Sarandon, her daughter Eva Amurri, Philippe Cassegrain
and Lucy Liu; Eva Mendes and Maggie Gyllenhaal.

Following pages, left to right:
The restroom, styled like a museum.
Overall view of the upper level.
The underside of the steel landscape, seen from the ground floor.

Thomas Heatherwick, a rising star of the Longchamp team

Designer Thomas Heatherwick is known in Great Britain for his creations that defy the laws of physics. His most emblematic works, each one more spectacular than the last, include a Japanese Buddhist temple inspired by folds of fabric, a sculptural starburst precariously balanced on a few spires in Manchester, and London's Rolling Bridge, which can be retracted into an octagon-shaped sculpture.

Thomas Heatherwick trained at the Royal College of Art and founded his eponymous studio in 1994. Today a team of forty-five which includes architects, designers, engineers and makers work on project ranging from large-scale architectural schemes to products, furniture and large-scale works of public art.

Following the creation of La Maison Unique, he added new awards to an already strong list including the FX Award (2006), the *New York Construction Magazine Award* (2006), the AIA Award (2006) and the Talents du Luxe 2007 prize for exceptional talent in innovation.

Opposite: *B of the Bang* sculpture, Manchester, 2004.

Below: *The Pavilion of Ideas:* the project selected
to represent the United Kingdom at the Shanghai World Expo
in 2010.

Monsieur Philippe was a key part of the process. He contributed his boundless creativity, which Jean, in turn, tried to contain. His comments and points of view were always extremely relevant and ambitious, but he was also a stickler for detail, an absolute perfectionist with an incredible eye.

During a meeting in New York, the project team were all seated around the table…, when Monsieur Philippe arrived. It was impossible to make him sit down. He grabbed me by my sweater and pulled me upstairs to discuss the store layout. We had both marked out the layout with tape, to test our plans onsite. We were wondering where to install various items, and where we were going to place the staircase. I had this strange moment where everyone including Tom Chapman-Andrews, who led the scheme from the studio and Jean Cassegrain, were working extremely seriously, surrounded by computers, blueprints and drawings and I was kneeling on the floor with Monsieur Philippe, laying down the tape.

The meetings we had on the project were also unusual. For example, we had to use specialized suppliers for many elements including the magnets used to attach the merchandise display system to the steel ribbon structures. When I visited our manufacturer, he showed me his finger – which he had had plastic surgery on after the flesh had been torn off by an ultra-powerful magnet. When I brought his magnets to the meeting, there were some nervous looks and people were a little reluctant to touch the magnets… just in case they trapped their finger.

Not long before the opening, a rumor was going around that Jean's uncle Dominique had promised his friend Uma Thurman that there would be a crocodile toilet seat in the boutique. I think the team were unsure what I would think about the idea, so didn't tell whether the rumour was true or not, but Dominique had made a promised so they had it made in secret – in white crocodile – and installed it on the sly in the restroom reserved for customers. I think it's a great curiosity for the shop.

I was continually impressed by Jean's calm approach to such an ambitious architectural project – particularly when no one has ever done anything like it before. It was one of the most enjoyable projects my studio has ever delivered and much of that is down to the support and trust offered by the Cassegrain family. We developed close ties over that time. On the day of the opening when everyone else was rushing to prepare for the launch, Madame Cassegrain approached me and said: 'Thomas, remember that this place is your home – wherever you may be.' I was deeply touched."

Below: One of the first sketches of the Maison Unique.

Opposite: Detailed view of the upper level, where thin strips of the ash ceiling are curved down to the floor and transformed into display shelves.

Following pages: Central view of the steel staircase, dotted with magnetized display stands.
The steel landscape seen from the ground floor.
Detail of steel ribbons.

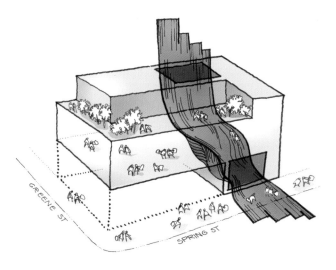

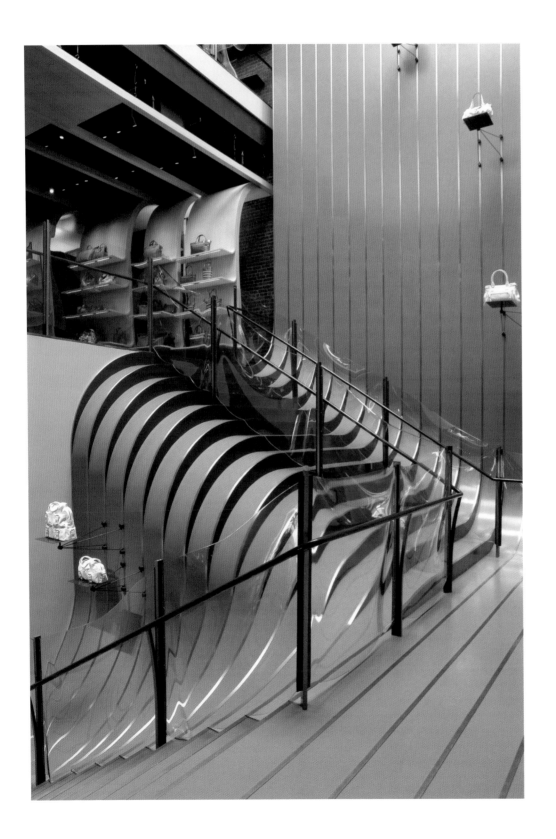

Olivier Cassegrain and the American challenge

As a teenager, Olivier Cassegrain had his doubts about joining Longchamp…, out of a desire to discover new horizons and "do something completely different." "But over time, you change…," and that's how the passion for leather goods caught up with the youngest of Philippe and Michèle Cassegrain's children.

Olivier Cassegrain joined the company in 1997, after five years of experience in the hotel industry. Longchamp's meteoric growth in the United States prompted him to go abroad to develop that market. Today he covers the country from coast to coast, setting up Longchamp shops and spurring on the brand's rapid expansion, just as his father did forty years earlier.

"At first, my training in the hotel industry doesn't appear to be related to my activity at Longchamp, but it's quite the opposite. A chain of stores requires a very similar dynamic, since the customer remains the common denominator in both cases.

I decided to go the States to develop our American branch when we opened our Madison Avenue store in 1999. Since then, we have opened an average of one store per year, while simultaneously building up our American office to support this sustained development.

Thanks to this rapid commercial expansion, the Longchamp name is becoming more and more familiar to the public. We also endeavor to be absolutely beyond reproach in the services we offer our clientele, particularly in terms of after sales service, with the goal of providing quality customer service at all levels.

Occasionally, people say: "It's amazing how much Longchamp has changed!" But I have the feeling that the company has always been on the move. We're driven to excel at what we do. Longchamp has been changing and evolving for years."

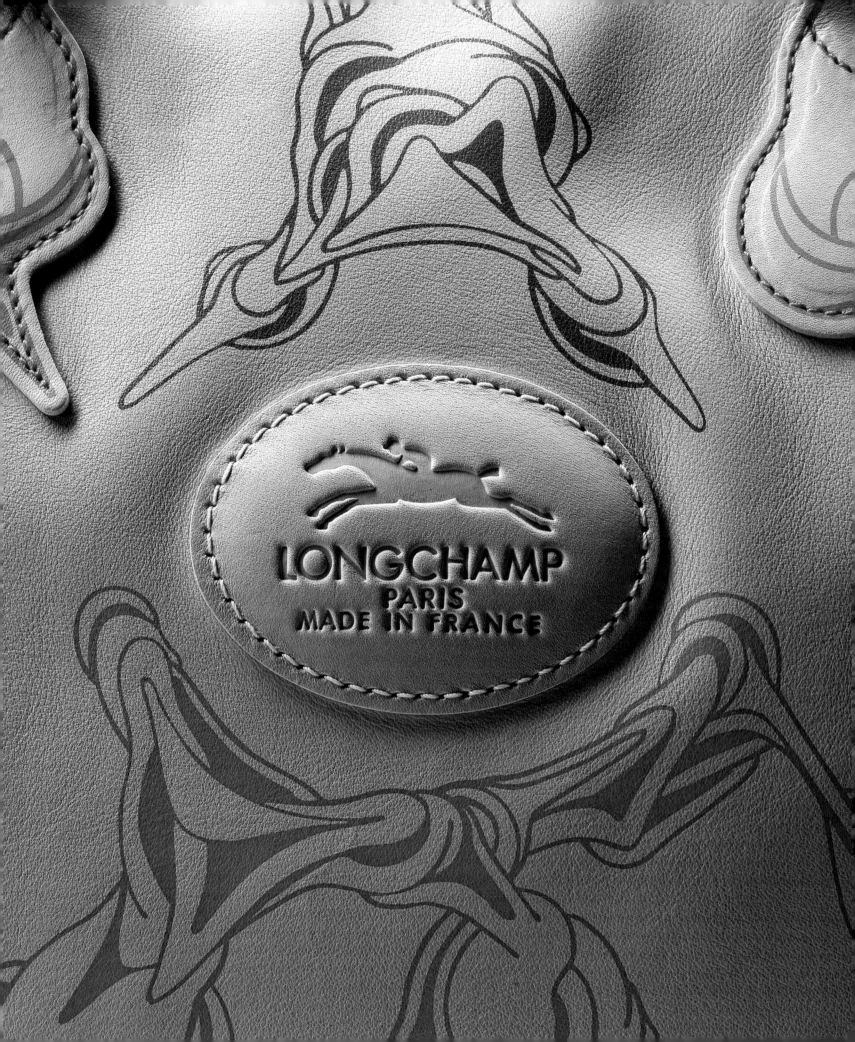

Bags, as accessories, were becoming quite the fashion statement. It was hard to resist the desire to unfold it, varnish it, enlarge it, perforate it, color it, embroider it, and zip it back up and then unzip it again. But where straight-laced fashion fell short, Longchamp's creativity wisely took an innovative approach, surprisingly using leathers and fabrics as an artistic expression. Was it Art with a capital A? Perhaps it was closer to an artistic pursuit – about which the company preferred to remain somewhat discreet, while spicing up its designs with a hint of aesthetic whimsy borrowed from the art world.

As early as 1971, Jean Cassegrain invited the painter Serge Mendjiski to work on bags cut from lambskin, the new leather he was developing for his collections at the time. Mendjiski, the herald of the artistic movement Divisionism, expressed himself on leather as he did on canvas – by dividing up his material. The zodiac-themed products created by the artist were ornamented with a leather patchwork design, whose colored squares only took on meaning from a certain angle.

Even though Longchamp delights in creating surprise by offering the most explosive creative minds the opportunity to express themselves in its products, these initiatives must not be mistaken for an artificial quest for attention from the art world. The Cassegrain family has always supported fashion and the arts. They have never been willing to create the illusion of intellectual interests or to nurture a pompous reputation as a *patron of the arts*. Friendship has never been measured by the effect of public relations campaigns. Longchamp avoids excessive marketing tactics, as sincerity is part of the company's culture. For example, the painter Gen Paul, a well-known figure in Montmartre during the 1950s, created several gouache paintings for his friend Dominique Cassegrain, to serve as backgrounds for Longchamp display windows. The artwork was accompanied by an impromptu "lesson" in presentation techniques, which were then religiously adhered to by Dominique.

As the company's style evolved, it pushed its creations to previously unknown limits. Each project was more daring than the last, and was unique. Longchamp enjoys shaking the foundations of traditional functional products, preferring to work on novel creations, thus blurring the boundaries between the arts, fashion and craftsmanship. Moreover, the Cassegrain family never cites the renowned artists who have enhanced their bags with their artistic visions without duly acknowledging the technical challenges involved. For its fiftieth anniversary, the company invited several artists to create the bag of their dreams – thus initiating a brief media foray into the world of stars. The creations included: a bag for musical scores and a violin case for musicians Anne-Lise Gastaldi and David Lefèvre, a bag designed to hold the plans and drawing boards of decorator Patrice Nourissat, a tutu bag for

Preceding page: Detail from one of the sixty "Moerman Original" bags produced for the sixtieth anniversary of Longchamp.

Below: The canvas and calfskin architect's bag designed by decorator Patrice Nourissat for the fiftieth anniversary of the firm.

Opposite: Lambskin bag decorated with a leather mosaic created by artist Serge Mendjiski on the sign of the zodiac, *Pisces*, 1971.

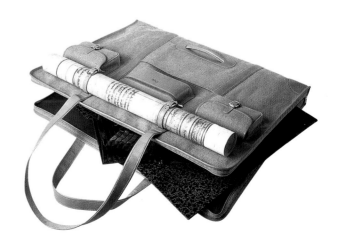

Opposite, from left to right and from top to bottom:
Gold Card, *Poodle* and *Stomp*: the *Pliage* bags
conceived by designer Jeremy Scott (Fall-Winter 2008-2009,
Fall-Winter 2007-2008, Spring-Summer 2008).

Below: The *Zip Bag* designed by Thomas Heatherwick
in 2004.

ballet dancer Agnès Letestu, and numerous others – all incredible works that still arouse deep emotion at the Segré workshops, whose skill and craftsmanship were strongly put to the test at the time!

And then there was the "impossible" bag devised by British designer Thomas Heatherwick in 2004. Well before he was asked by Jean Cassegrain to design the Maison Unique in New York, Heatherwick suggested that Longchamp create a bag composed of nothing more than a zipper – wound up in a spiral – which, when unzipped, resulted in a surprising amount of space. Longchamp was impressed by his proposal, but wondered: was this *ever-so-British eccentricity* even feasible to produce? The company's response was: yes, if we work at it. And work at it they did, with boundless energy, and then some. A year of more or less successful attempts was required to successfully roll up the zipper into its spiraled vortex: a full year of research to arrive at a conclusive prototype. It was an "adventure" in the truest sense of the word. Thomas Heatherwick's striking, ingenious *Zip Bag* finally emerged from the workshops in a range of dual color schemes designed to highlight its modular construction.

The *Zip Bag* by Thomas Heatherwick

"My old studio was located nearby a zip factory. I'd heard that they sold enormous rolls of zip in lengths up to 200 meters and was curious about what you could make from such a long piece of zip. I wondered whether it could be used to make a handbag and worked with my team to make a prototype that could be taken to a manufacturer. That's when I discovered Longchamp – I immediately felt a strong affinity for the brand because the quality of its products was so strong, and it had substantial expertise as a manufacturer of luxury leather goods.

I visited Paris and presented my idea to Monsieur Philippe, Jean and Sophie. As they listened to me present my idea, I had the feeling that they were initially a bit puzzled about who I was. But quickly they understood the concept and quite quickly we began to work together on developing the prototype further.

It typically takes only two weeks to create a prototype for a handbag… our project took over a year because of the need for a detailed knowledge of engineering. The bag's style was not the main problem; the real challenge was technical in nature. I made regular trips to Segré to meet with the teams in charge of the project. Everyone worked very diligently on the creation of the bag… and eventually on its production.

When it was launched, the *Zip Bag* was very well received. I was quite shocked when I heard how well it was selling in Japan, Germany, Australia and even in Korea. Throughout the process Longchamp impressed me with their determination and willingness to explore new ground and make new relationships."

When Longchamp contacted controversial "Britartist" Tracey Emin the same year to produce a limited edition bag to commemorate the tenth anniversary of *Le Pliage*, the company took another major risk. The English artist – well known for her embroidery work, which tends to be as candid and introspective as a private diary – hand sews floral fabrics to express recurrent themes from her personal experience. Poisonous flowers and naively shaped letters are quilted in an irregular way, making them very difficult to reproduce with accuracy. It was also important to respect the exact shape of the various elements, such as the pointed petals, which symbolize *fleurs du mâle* in the artist's fertile imagination, where *mal* (evil) is associated with *mâle* (male). Longchamp concentrated on the technical aspect, investing a huge sum in the project without knowing how it would be received by the public. They needn't have worried: customers were spellbound. They were delighted to possess a totally unique handbag – which was also a small work of art, signed by the artist's hand – a temptation that was hard to resist.

Below: Portrait of Emmanuelle Béart carrying her *Tracey Emin for Longchamp* bag, *Elle* magazine, 2005.

Opposite: Portrait of artist Tracey Emin with the first example of the bag *International woman me every time*, which she created for Longchamp.

Opposite, from top to bottom and from left to right:
Jeremy Scott and his travel case *This is not your bag*,
in May 2006.
Duffel bag from the *Garden Foo* collection designed
by the Me Company collective.
Jean Cassegrain and Michel Gaubert at the launch
of the *MG by Longchamp* collection in Tokyo in March 2008.

The same technical issues were called into play when the London-based design studio, Me Company, was invited to collaborate on a bag in the summer of 2006. While the cylinder printing of fabric is ordinarily limited to eight colors, the design studio delivered a prototype which, in theory, was impossible to produce. The *Garden Foo* collection used over a thousand colors, which needed to be reproduced on 50,000 feet of cloth! Longchamp spent long hours on this insanely difficult task, solicited assistance from its suppliers, and developed its own technical resources to meet the artistic demands. Their relentless efforts paid off in the end. The psychedelic vines of *Garden Foo* have spread their shoots throughout shops the world over.

The signature works of sophisticated artists were thus added to the company's collections without raising an eyebrow. Designer Jeremy Scott, a friend of the company, has been enthusiastically creating innovatively designed luggage for several seasons. He made a sensational debut with a collection stamped: *This is not your bag*. The American designer had great fun imitating the look of wooden crates used for ocean freight.
The company's latest artistic foray concerns the music world. Sound designer Michel Gaubert recently designed a mini-collection (MG by Longchamp) dedicated to the world of music – ranging from an iPod case to a travel *Case* for DJs – featuring a facetiously designed printed fabric inspired by the 1980s – a tribute to old audio cassettes and *ghetto blasters* used by breakdancers.
The collection is right in step with the latest trends, while not being overly "trendy" – and therein lies the secret.

Sixty years of constant renewal...

To celebrate the company's sixtieth anniversary, the legendary *LM* bag designed by Philippe Cassegrain at the beginning of the 1970s has returned to the limelight. After winning the hearts of elegant Japanese ladies, for whom the bag was originally designed, an identical replica was created as a collector's item, revived from Longchamp's prestigious past for a single season. This new edition was also accompanied by newly designed creations, in order to more firmly anchor this legacy of the past in Longchamp's contemporary artistic current.

Evoking the company's history, the project was also intended as a declaration of love to those women without whom Longchamp would never have embodied French excellence, and as a statement of respect for its partners, who seek out the rarest materials, spare no effort to deliver faultless craftsmanship, and instinctively understand what "Longchamp" signifies.

The new *LM* handbag is a bridge linking two eras. The suppliers of old were still there when needed. In the 1970s, Alain and Philippe Cassegrain decided to develop their "dream leather" in collaboration with the Tanneries Haas, in Alsace. The calfskin was tanned in its natural state and then silk-screened, a process decried as sacrilege by some. The tannery, founded near Strasbourg in 1842, has developed an exceptional level of expertise over successive generations, works with premium calf leather from animals raised in France. The technical development of this patterned leather required long hours of meticulous adjustments.

Nearly forty years later, Jean Cassegrain and Sophie Delafontaine called upon the firm to supply them with leather. And Jean-Christophe Muller, who represents the sixth generation of the Tanneries Haas, dutifully rose to the challenge once again, using today's techniques.

Below: Black patent *LM* travel bag and black vintage *LM* tote bag, new 2008 edition.

Opposite: Vintage *LM* travel bag, new 2008 edition.

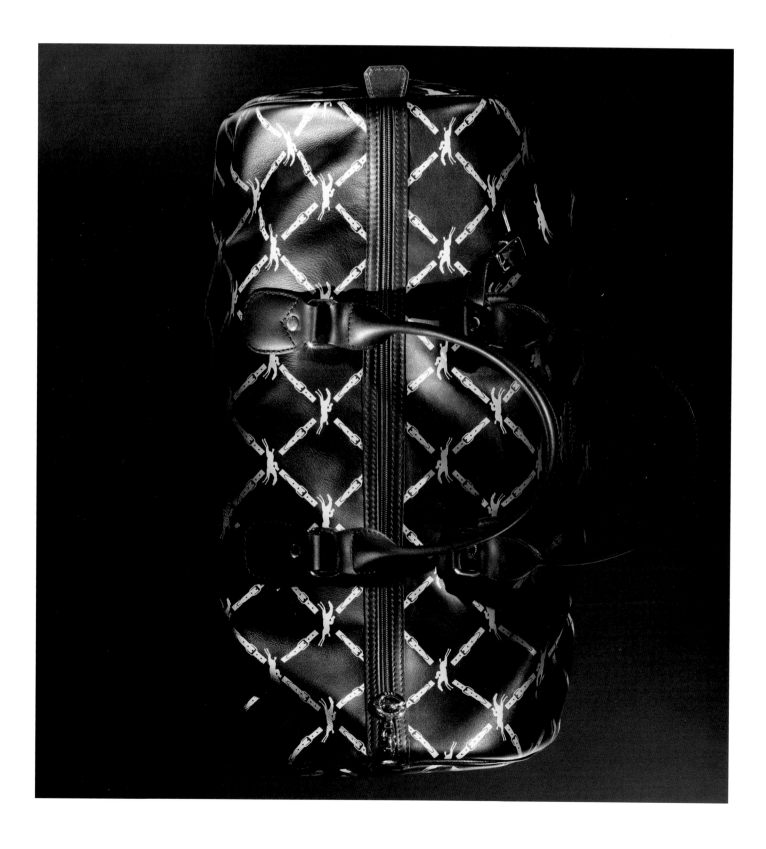

The "Moerman Edition"

For the new version of the *LM* handbag, Longchamp turned to the organic line drawings of Belgian artist Jean-Luc Moerman to adorn the bag's classic curves. The artist, who was born in 1967, creates abstract forms inspired by the techniques of tattooing, graffiti and mangas, which completely invade the media on which he works – somewhat like a virus. He doesn't hesitate to incorporate new technologies and scientific advances into his work, drawing infinitely complicated shapes that seem to quiver with life. His polymorphous work has been popular with collectors of contemporary art for over 15 years, particularly in Japan, the United States and Europe.

For the *LM*, Moerman devised invasive convoluted forms, which were tattooed directly on the leather, just as a tattoo is applied to someone's skin. The project, which was christened the "Moerman Edition", features a monochromatic design on a flesh-colored leather background. Sixty *LM* bags were also entrusted to the artist so that he could express himself directly on the medium. This line – known as the "Moerman Original" collection – represents a symbolic gesture for Longchamp, summing up the very essence of its craft with humor and vision.

Opposite, left: *Neon Light* by Jean-Luc Moerman, 2005.

Opposite, right: *LM* bag reinterpreted
by Jean-Luc Moerman for Longchamp's sixtieth anniversary.

Opposite: The New Year's card created
by Chéri Samba in 2007.

Below: The New Year's card created
by Robert Combas in 1994.

Following pages: Free interpretation of a catalog page
by Robert Combas in 1997.
Invitation card created by Paella Chimicos for
the opening of the boutique in the rue du Vieux-Colombier
in Paris on September 17, 1993.

Dominique Cassegrain, a lover of the arts

After years devoted to expanding the distribution of Longchamp products, Dominique Cassegrain decided to discretely withdraw from the venture. He remains nonetheless a discoverer of visionary talent and an adviser to Philippe, Jean and Sophie throughout the collaborative artistic projects conducted by the company. Each year, he also devotes himself to the search for new artists to produce the celebrated Longchamp New Year's cards. In 1990, Stéphane Trois Carrés painted a canvas cut up into 650 squares. The contemporary creators who have tried their hand at this perilous exercise include Velikovic (1991), Segui (2005), Robert Combas (1995), Miss-Tic (2001), Tony Soulié (2000), and Cheri Samba (2007).

Like any self-respecting collector, Dominique shuns the politically correct. Some may consider that a photo of a lonely trailer in a desolate landscape is chilling to accompany the traditional season's greetings of prosperity: no doubt the generally accepted view. But is that sufficient reason to rule it out? Such conventional views are not part and parcel of the Cassegrain clan's resilient character. The photo of the trailer, signed by Pierre Ardouvin, was acclaimed despite the hesitation of conformists. Amazingly, this choice coincided with the perfume of scandal which had recently cast its spell over Jean and Sophie. The air of the times was leading to unorthodox thinking. The new advertising campaign, featuring Kate Moss scoffing at her banishment, provoked heated debate in the media. But Longchamp demonstrated its conviction, acting on the principle that conventions are made to be transgressed.

-DEPUIS QU'ELLE AVAIT APPRIS L'
d'effeuiller ses calendriers jus
Qu'à LA DATE FATIDIQUE X
PAELLA CHIMICOS 93

Sixty years and going strong!

As one chapter in the company's history closes, the next is already emerging under the continuing creative inspiration of the Cassegrain family.

"Although certain characteristics have been preserved by the continuity provided by the family, that has not prevented the company from 'moving with the times'. On the contrary, Longchamp's ability to continuously call itself into question and reinvent itself is an integral part of its genetic code.

I sometimes wonder what my grandfather would think of Longchamp today… I hope he would be proud of what his enterprise has become. But I'm not sure he would really be surprised by the distance traveled. The values which he instilled in Longchamp constitute the cornerstone of our work: the search for quality, a sense of innovation and an international perspective. Over the years, we have simply deployed these values in other areas. In short, even though everything has evolved, nothing has changed."

Jean Cassegrain, 2008.

Preceding pages: The New Year's card painted by Vladimir Velickovic in 1991.

Opposite: Black patent *LM* English bag, new 2008 edition.

Marie Aucouturier would like to warmly thank:

Philippe and Michèle Cassegrain, Jean Cassegrain and Sophie Delafontaine
for their confidence in her;
Alain Cassegrain, Brigitte Cassegrain, Jean-François Cassegrain and
Dominique Cassegrain, all unparalleled "tellers" of the Longchamp story;
Luc Frémont and the employees of the Segré plant, who welcomed her
with patience and kindness;

The following *Pliage* enthusiasts: Sylvie and Solenne Revier,
Agathe Roussillon, Martine and Véronique Jenny, Maylis Hay,
Delphine Deleval and Christine Bordon;
As well as the *Pliage* expert, Elyette Roux;

Nathalie Mayevski and Corinne Schmidt, without whom this book would
have never come to be;
Alexandra Ilievski, an experienced investigator;

Matthieu, her other *plume*.

Philippe Garcia would like to thank:

For their confidence, hospitality and advice: the Cassegrain family,
Luc Frémont and all the personnel of Segré.

For their participation and enthusiasm: Marie-Christine Goux, Marie and
Philippe de la Bâthie, Aude Perrier and Georges, Laurence Tordjman and
Anya, Bertrand Raynaud, Isabelle Bardot, Victorine, Aurélien Storny,
Francesca, Livia, Elena Van der Stay and Alex Tharreau.

And finally, Odile Horion, Nathalie Mayevski and Corinne Schmidt
of the Éditions de la Martinière.

Photographic credits

The publisher would like to thank the Heritage Department of Air France, as well as all others
who were gracious enough to lend us their documents.

P. 11, 14, 15, 16, 22, 23, 24, 25 : © Philippe Garcia. P. 13, 17, 18, 21, 26 : © Longchamp archives.
P. 19 : Elvis image used by permission, Elvis Presley Enterprises, Inc./DR.
P. 31, 34 : © Philippe Garcia. P. 32, 33, 35, 36bl, 37, 39, 41, 42 : © Longchamp archives.
P. 36 br : © Alex Tharreau. P. 38 : © Odette Baumont/DR.
P. 47, 51, 52, 53 : © Philippe Garcia. P. 49 : © Roger-Viollet. P. 50 : © Daniel Aron.
P. 52, 53 : ADP/Paul Andreu – © Adagp, Paris 2008.
P. 54, 55, 56 : © Longchamp archives. P. 58 : © Musée Air France Collection/DR.
P. 63, 65, 66, 68, 69, 75t : © Philippe Garcia. P. 64, 67, 70, 74, 75b, 76 : © Longchamp archives.
P. 71, 73 : © Ken Griffith. P. 72 : © Daniel Jouanneau/Model Rachel Riley.
P. 81, 84t, 85, 98 : © Philippe Garcia. P. 82, 84b : © Longchamp archives. P. 83 : DR.
P. 87 : © Nicolas Bruant. P. 88-89 : © Dimitri Tolstoï. P. 91 : © Daniel Aron. P. 92, 93, 94, 95 : © Alex Tharreau.
P. 103, 106, 107, 108, 109, 110, 112, 113, 114, 116, 117, 118 : © Philippe Garcia. P. 105 : © Longchamp archives.
P. 123, 124t, 127, 130, 138, 141, 142 : © Philippe Garcia. P. 124b : © Longchamp archives.
P. 125 : © Philippe Lacombe. P. 126 : © Daniel Aron. P. 128, 129 : © Longchamp archives/Model Georgina Stojiljkovic.
P. 131 : © Andrea Klarin/Model Katia Z. P. 132-133 : © Miles Aldridge/Model Lily Cole.
P. 135, 136-137 : © Mario Sorrenti/Model Kate Moss. P. 139 : © Andrea Herzog/Stylist Luc Rasori/Model Reine Grave.
P. 140 : © Robert Jaso/Model Christina Ionno.
P. 147, 148, 152, 153, 157, 158, 160-161, 162 : © Adrian Wilson. P. 150-151 : © Patrick McMullen.
P. 154t : © Markn Ogue. P. 154b : © Jon Super/AP/SIPA. P. 155, 156 : © Heatherwick Studio. P. 159 : © Longchamp archives.
P. 167, 171, 178t, 179, 189 : © Philippe Garcia. P. 168 : © Nicolas Bruant. P. 169 : © Alex Tharreau.
P. 170t : © Jean-Pierre Salle. P. 170bl : © Jean-Jacques Collot. P. 170br : © Olivier Mesnage.
P. 172 : © Emanuele Scorcelletti/Gamma for Elle. P. 173 : © Mary McCartney. P. 174t : © Longchamp archives/AGC.
P. 174br, 180, 181, 182, 183, 184-185, 186-187 : © Longchamp archives. P. 178b : © Philippe D.

First published in 2008 by Éditions de La Martinière, Paris

Cataloging-in-Publication Data has been applied for and may be obtained from the Library of Congress.
ISBN: 978-0-8109-2107-8

Copyright © 2008 Éditions de La Martinière, an imprint of La Martinière Groupe, Paris

Printed and bound in France
10 9 8 7 6 5 4 3 2 1

HNA
harry n. abrams, inc.
a subsidiary of La Martinière Groupe

115 West 18th Street
New York, NY 10011
www.hnabooks.com